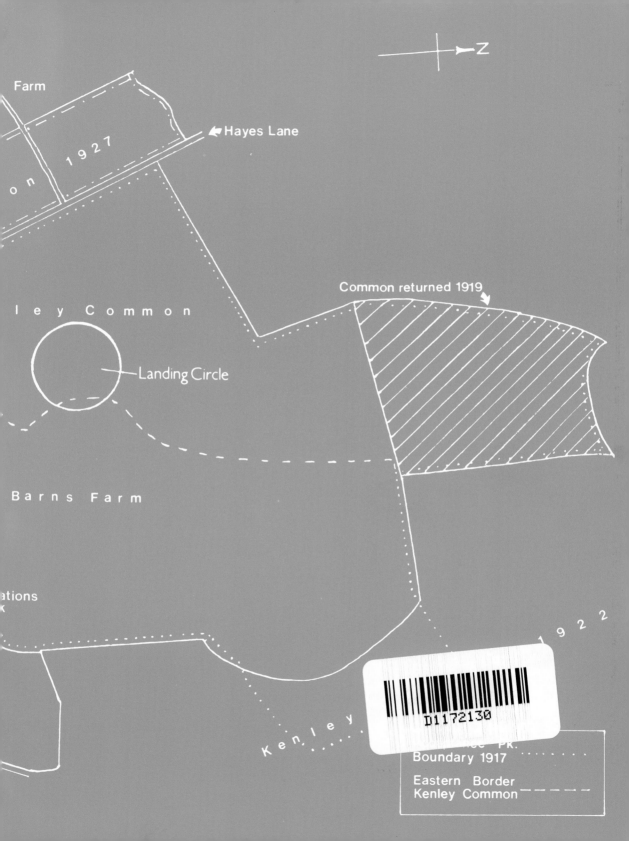

Farm

1927

◄ Hayes Lane

l e y   C o m m o n

Common returned 1919

Landing Circle

B a r n s   F a r m

ations

K e n l e y

1 9 2 2

D1172130

Pk.
Boundary 1917   · · · · · · · ·

Eastern Border
Kenley Common   — · — · — ·

358
.417
F62

7/2013

R.A.F. KENLEY

Hawker Demons of No 23 Squadron, which was at Kenley from 1927 to 1932.   *Flight*

R.A.F. KENLEY

The Story of the Royal Air Force Station 1917–1974

by

PETER FLINT

Foreword by
Air Chief Marshal Sir Theodore McEvoy, K.C.B., C.B.E.

TERENCE DALTON LIMITED
LAVENHAM . SUFFOLK
1985

Published by
TERENCE DALTON LIMITED

ISBN 0 86138 036 3

Text photoset in 11/12 pt Baskerville

Printed in Great Britain at
The Lavenham Press Limited, Lavenham, Suffolk

© Peter Flint 1985

Contents

The royalties from this book are being paid directly to the Blond McIndoe Centre for Medical Research at the Queen Victoria Hospital, East Grinstead. The hospital, where Sir Archibald McIndoe and his team restored the faces and bodies of many R.A.F. aircrew who had suffered severe burns when their aircraft were shot down, was "adopted" by the personnel of R.A.F. Kenley during the Second World War.

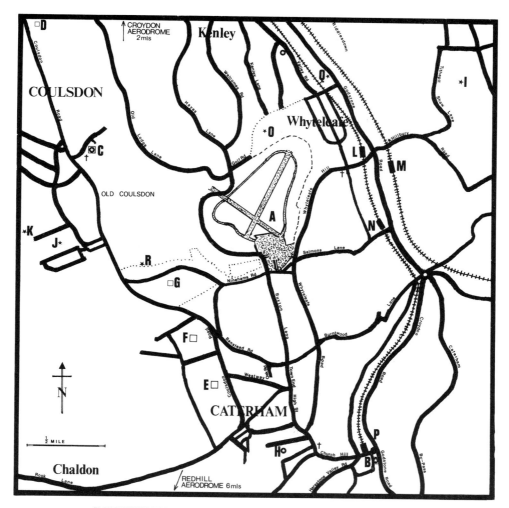

PLAN SHOWING AN APPROXIMATION OF PLACES AND EVENTS RELEVANT TO KENLEY AERODROME

A	Aerodrome	F	Caterham Barracks	M	Upper Warlingham Station
B	Camp B, Emergency Operations Room Butcher's Shop	G	Coulsdon Common	N	Whyteleafe South Station
		H	Queens Park	O	Kenley Common
C	Camp C, "The Grange" Operations Room	I	Batts Farm	P	Caterham Station
		J	Tollers Farm	Q	Rose and Crown Public House
D	Coulsdon Court Golf Course Club House. Mess	K	Farthing Downs	R	Windmill Farm
E	St. Lawrence's Hospital	L	Whyteleafe Station		

A sketch map of the Kenley area showing the position of Kenley aerodrome.

Acknowledgements

NO BOOK of this nature can be written without the help of many people, and it has been my good fortune to have been particularly blessed in this respect.

Norman and Peggy Bray served in the Operations Room during the Second World War and so were able to supply much information about it, and about its re-location to Caterham and Old Coulsdon. Time spent with them at their home, not far from "The Grange" where once they were a part of the team that controlled Hurricanes and Spitfires, was always informative and a pleasure. Cliff Kenyon, one of their colleagues who also lives nearby, helped with this period. Reg Sheldrake was at the aerodrome several years before, and during, the Second World War and recalled in great detail what life was like.

Gene Roux lived his early days in Kenley Lane, not far from the aerodrome, and enlisted with No 615 Squadron prior to the outbreak of war in 1939. Now resident in Australia, he sent many extracts from his personal diaries which were of considerable value. Gene, who had earlier been "booked" by the Metropolitan Police for riding his unlicensed motor-cycle in Croydon while on leave, was surprised to find that the law had caught up with him while he was with the squadron in France. His Commanding Officer, Squadron Leader J. R. Kayll, advised him to write an apology, and nothing further was heard; I am also indebted to Squadron Leader Kayll, D.S.O., D.F.C., O.B.E., for his help. Group Captain Peter Simpson, D.S.O., D.F.C., devoted much time to corresponding with me about the air raid of 18th August, 1940; Squadron Leader Harry Newton also gave assistance here. Group Captain Tom Gleave offered advice and information from his own records, as I tried to put together the picture of that traumatic day during the Battle of Britain. It was while he was researching his book *The Hardest Day* which deals exclusively with the events of 18th August, 1940, that I came into contact with Alfred Price, the renowned aviation writer and historian; it was through our exchange of information that I learnt much of the German view of the raid.

My thanks are due to Andrew Cormack and his colleagues at the Royal Air Force Museum, Hendon; also E. A. Munday and the people of the Air Historical Branch of the Royal Air Force, Theobalds Road, London. The staff of Local Studies Sections of the libraries at Purley and Caterham Valley were always friendly and helpful. J. J. Halley of *Air Britain* kindly supplied the list of squadrons based at Kenley.

It would have been impossible to produce such an account as this without recourse to the photographic collections of Surrey County

Libraries, and pictures from this source are reproduced with the kind permission of Surrey County Library Local Studies Librarian. Equally valuable has been the permission of the Trustees of the Imperial War Museum to use wartime photographs from the collections at Lambeth.

John Setter, a member of the Caterham branch of the Royal Air Forces Association and member of their Portcullis Club, has lived near the aerodrome all his life and consequently knows every inch of it; knowledge he kindly imparted to me. Other members of the club were equally accommodating.

Barry H. Abraham has done much research on First World War aircraft factories and was very helpful with general information of this period.

My good friend Tony Cook has been instrumental in assisting me in prodding the manuscript into shape by his constructive suggestions and wise counselling.

Charles Hall ("Holly") has made a very pleasing job of the illustration for the front cover, and I am also most grateful for the permission given by the artist and by Air Vice-Marshal K. W. Hayr, Air Officer Commanding No 11 Group, for me to use Lilian Buchanan's painting "Our Wing Engaged" on the back cover. This was painted in the Kenley Operations Room at "The Grange" during 1943 and 1944.

To everyone not mentioned above who has been associated with the writing of this book, from those supplying snippets of information to those writing reminiscences, which are its backbone, I give my most grateful thanks.

Air Chief Marshal Sir Theodore McEvoy, K.C.B., C.B.E., when serving at Kenley as an Air Commodore, did a large amount of work on a Station history which he was unable to complete before being moved on. The results of his labours he generously passed on to me; without this and his continued help and encouragement over the years, this book would never have been written. I am also deeply indebted to him for writing the Foreword.

My greatest help and counsellor has been my wife, Iris, who has been both secretary and typist, showing great tolerance when her concentration has been regularly diverted from household affairs to ponder on more important things like "How do you think this paragraph reads?"

Transcripts of Crown copyright records (AIR28/419, AIR50/92, AIR1/1040/204/5/1470 and AIR1/452/15/312/26) in the Public Record Office appear by permission of the Controller of H.M. Stationery Office.

Rickman Hill,   Peter Flint
Coulsdon,
Surrey. 1985

Foreword

By Air Chief Marshal Sir Theodore McEvoy, K.C.B., C.B.E.

A S AIR Officer Commanding, 61 Group, in 1950, I wrote to all the distinguished people who had been connected with Kenley from its beginnings, asking for their reminiscences, meaning to compile a brief history of the Station to interest future "inmates". I was posted away before I could make further headway and the project lapsed.

Now Peter Flint has not only used those reminiscences but has done a first-class job of research resulting in this history, in a way I could not have hoped to do myself. As far as I can see it is without fault. The greater part of the story naturally concerns the Battle of Britain: it brings out vividly and in a movingly personal way the terrible losses we suffered and shows what a "damned close-run thing" it was.

I strongly recommend this history, particularly, of course, to those in Surrey who have been inconvenienced and preserved by the Royal Air Force and to all who are interested in the beginnings and development of the flying Services.

Rowledge
1985

Introduction

WHEN, in 1917, the first aeroplane took to the air from what a few days earlier had been Kenley Common, no one could have foreseen that those few acres of land were destined to become a centre of military aviation for a period which was to span nearly three decades, almost the entire era of piston-engined, propeller-driven fighters. During those years most of the country's front-line machines were resident at one time or another, the most memorable being the Hurricane and the Spitfire.

The history of the Station has been essentially about people; people from all walks of life and of all nationalities. To a large degree, it has also encompassed citizens residing in the surrounding district, whose lives have not been without incident, particularly during the early days when aero-engines were something less than reliable and throughout the Second World War. From their witness of past events, Kenley people, both Royal Air Force personnel and "locals", have helped me to create a picture of Kenley which I hope is worthy of what was once one of the country's foremost fighter stations and home of "the Few".

Kenley aerodrome from the south-east in 1950, showing the remaining hangar with Avro Ansons on the apron.

CHAPTER ONE

Aeroplanes on the Common

CONWAY JENKINS' interest in aviation developed during its very early days, at the time when the progress of aeroplane design can be attributed as much to the elementary principle of trial and error as to anything else. When the *Daily Mail* put up £10,000 prize money at Brooklands for a Circuit of Britain air race in 1911 Conway Jenkins had already learned to fly, and he persuaded the brilliant designer Robert Blackburn to allow him to pilot one of his Mercury monoplanes.

His contribution to the success of the race was very small and opinions on how he came to grief are varied: one view is that the aileron wires on the machine had somehow become crossed, causing him to crash while taking off; another suggests that he finished upside down after being blown over while taxi-ing out for the start. Either way, his participation in the event was not altogether successful, but it did show him to be an aviator of some importance.

In 1914 Jenkins moved home to "Glen Cottage" in Hillbury Road, down in the valley at Whyteleafe, and by the outbreak of war he was, no doubt, fully acquainted with the topography of the local landscape, a latent knowledge which he was to use to good effect later on.

At the outbreak of hostilities the serious manufacture of aeroplanes in Britain was confined to a handful of small companies who, although possessing considerable talents, were unable due to their size to produce anything like the requirement of a country that had just embarked upon a full-scale war. As military experience was gained and an even greater awareness of the potential of the aeroplane as a weapon emerged, a mass production process became essential and the Military Aeronautics Directorate at the War Office embarked upon a policy of obtaining minutely detailed drawings of aircraft approved by the Royal Aircraft Factory at Farnborough and contracting the work to companies not previously associated with aviation. This scheme was organised under the direct tutelage and inspection of the men from Farnborough.

The well-established aeroplane manufacturing companies were already gearing themselves up to a programme of rapid expansion, with

Bristol Fighters of No 24 Squadron practising for the 1921 R.A.F. Pageant, with Old Lower Warlingham golf course below.
Air Chief Marshal Sir James Robb

large contracts in their pockets and the promise of a rewarding future. They were also receiving revenue from the use of their designs by other companies who were manufacturing the types under licence. Later, when the manufacturing programme was ticking over and properly organised, the outpourings from the various sources amounted to a considerable number of aeroplanes.

To cope with the increasing volume of machines entering service with the Royal Flying Corps, the system whereby they were received and prepared for active service was expanded. New aerodromes, or Aircraft Acceptance Parks, were hastily constructed for this specific purpose. Their sphere of operation was large and diverse, from testing completed machines received from aeroplane companies to assembling components manufactured by sub-contractors into the final product. Wings, fuselage, tailplane, etc., were made by one company, engines by another, instruments, wheels and other minor assemblies by various others. Some companies completed their machines and flew them in from fields adjacent to the works, but in the main they arrived in crates by road and rail.

The testing and tuning of all machines was in the hands of experienced pilots of the Aeronautical Inspection Department, and it was only after they had given flight clearance that the machines were accepted as being up to the required standard for the front line squadrons. It was these test pilots who made the decision either to accept machines or to reject them for improvements to be made.

Conway Jenkins had proved himself an efficient organiser with the Army Service Corps, and when someone was required to set up the Acceptance Parks he transferred and started work at Hendon. This proved so successful that he soon had five hundred men under his command; he was made a major, with a relative rise in pay. This correlation of numbers of men to rank and pay qualified him for a rapid rise in rank and fortune comparable to his expanding command, and its significance was not lost on him.

While the search for further aerodrome sites was in progress, Conway Jenkins, promoted to lieutenant-colonel and Assistant Director of Aircraft Equipment, exercised his knowledge of the land with which he was most familiar; it was to the delightful Kenley Common, with its golf course wandering among little spinneys and beautiful trees, that he turned his appraising eye. To the experienced airman the fact that it was on high ground, which would prove beneficial in foggy weather, and had the added advantage of having easily acquirable farmland adjoining it, made the Common an attractive prospect. It is not difficult to visualise him standing in his garden casting a thoughtful glance at the high ground to the west of his home in the valley. It was almost certainly his influence that decided the fate of Kenley Common and its environs for many years to come.

It would appear that the first indication that local people had of the presence of an aerodrome on their doorstep was when a group of men appeared and surprisingly started felling trees and clearing scrub from the Common, a shock they shared with the Keeper, who was also totally unaware of Royal Flying Corps intentions.

The public outcry that followed eventually reached such proportions that questions were asked in Parliament. In a debate on 5th June, 1917, Sir F. Banbury, M.P., asked the Under Secretary for War, Mr Macpherson, whether he was aware that the R.F.C. had taken possession of eighty-one acres of Kenley Common and that they were in the process of cutting down eighty-year-old trees on land that the City of London was under statutory obligation to maintain for the use of the public. He further asked whether the Under Secretary was also aware that no notice was given to the Corporation of the intention of the Military to occupy the land, and said that they had first found out about such activities

The beginning: tents and Bessonneaux hangars in a field beside the Old Hayes Lane (centre). To the left can be seen the first stages in the construction of the permanent sheds. *Lieutenant-Colonel F. A. G. Noel*

through their Keeper (apparently when the Keeper had asked the officer in charge what was going on, he was curtly told that the land was being taken under the Defence of the Realm Act and the officer was going to do what he liked). Banbury finished his questions by asking whether the open space at nearby Farthing Down and several other sites had been considered for the purpose.

Sir Stuart Coates, M.P., also expressed indignation at the manner in which the land had been occupied without prior consultation and, like his fellow objectors, suggested alternative locations. He went on, "It is just possible that there is one reason that explains the taking of Kenley Common. I am informed that the Commanding Officer has his house so close to the Common that it will be infinitely more convenient for him to use the aerodrome at Kenley Common than any of the open spaces to which I have referred." (A direct, if erroneous, reference to Conway Jenkins; he was not Commanding Officer.)

In reply, the Under Secretary explained that it had been decided to take over the land and use it as an Acceptance Park and aerodrome for the purpose of assisting in defence against hostile daylight raids. Both Farthing Down and Kenley Common had been examined by many skilled pilots and it had been concluded that no human skill, owing to its natural formation, would make the former suitable; the Common was the best and most desirable site near London for their purpose. He pointed out other advantages. It was on a main road and could be served by three local railway stations which had facilities for receiving and handling aeroplane components from contractors; it had a mains water supply; and electric feed cables were in close proximity. The work had to proceed as a matter of extreme national emergency.

Perhaps the most accurate and constructive criticism came from a local builder. In a letter to Captain Noel, the Commanding Officer, he wrote, "On one point I think you will fail, viz. drainage. Evidence will be forthcoming that in winter Kenley Common is often a quagmire and during the past two years men have played golf in water, and balls have disappeared into the soft clay. I know that I have gone to great expense with my new houses in sinking wells on the same level to carry off surface water that has lain on waterlogged land." This was a sound judgement; even today Hayes Lane is still dogged by drainage problems.

The *Croydon Advertiser* was in no doubt about its opinion of the dissenters. In its editorial of 16th June, it said, "It was surely a short-sighted and unintentionally unpatriotic frame of mind which caused the weak-kneed protest of last week against the taking over of Kenley Common by the military authorities . . . we are very glad also that the objections to the taking of the Common for aerial purposes proved futile, as all such attempts we trust and feel confident will do." This reaction is not altogether surprising when one considers that three days previously a strong force of German Gotha long-range bombers had successfully attacked London, causing much damage and the loss of 162 lives. Nearer home, Croydon had been bombed by Zeppelin L-14, Captain Alois Böcker, on the night of 13th October, 1915, when eleven

Lieutenant L.N. Hollinghurst (later Air Chief Marshal Sir Leslie Hollinghurst, G.B.E., K.C.B., D.F.C.) standing outside the Test and Despatch Office at Kenley in 1917.

Lieutenant-Colonel F. A. G. Noel

people were killed; on 23rd September, 1916, Captain Heinrich Mathy in L-31 had released four bombs over Purley which fell in the Hall Way area not far from Kenley. The mood of the general public was one of dismay and growing disquiet about the inadequacy of the air defences. Although there had been some success against the Zeppelins, the Gothas could be seen apparently roaming at will over Southern England, with little or no opposition. As for the taking of the Common, the initial sharp exchange of words between the Keeper of the Common and the Commanding Officer nicely summarised the situation: "he was going to do what he liked", and he did just that.

Lieutenant L. N. Hollinghurst, D.F.C., extreme right, with colleagues of the Kenley Aircraft Acceptance Park, 1918. *Air Chief Marshal Sir Leslie Hollinghurst*

Work on the aerodrome had begun early in June, 1917. In a letter to the General Officer Commanding-in-Chief, Eastern Command, dated 26th May, 1917, Conway Jenkins had written:

> I am directed to inform you that a detachment of the R.F.C. consisting of approximately 21 Officers, 2 Warrant Officers and 207 other ranks, will shortly proceed to Kenley for permanent duty at an aerodrome which is being established there. The first batch of personnel will arrive on Wednesday next, the 30th instant, and, as it has been ruled that the Detachment is to be accommodated under canvas until the Autumn of this year, I am to request that the necessary steps for the accommodation of the Detachment may be taken early, in order to be sure that no time is lost in the Detachment starting work after their arrival through delay with regard to camp arrangements.

While the interest of the public was focused on the swift and uncompromising snatch of the Common, the R.F.C. was busily taking over the adjoining land of New Barn Farm,* land on the southern border, plus quite a large area of Waterhouse Farm where it joined

---

*Coincidentally, the aerodrome at Croydon, a few miles away, was also built on a New Barn Farm.

Hayes Lane to the west. All became part of the aerodrome site and was taken under the Defence of the Realm Act; neither farmers nor local council had received prior warning.

It was in the fields along Hayes Lane that all the main activity first took place, and it gained momentum at a rapid rate. The camp mushroomed until eventually eighteen Bessonneaux* hangars and upwards of seventy bell tents, marquees and other portable buildings were standing on the site which only a few days earlier had been farmland. In a matter of days the first aeroplane was completed and tested; work was well ahead of schedule.

The continuing use of Hayes Lane by the public caused the R.F.C. its biggest headache. The normal traffic of local people going about their daily business soon became augmented by an ever-increasing flow of sightseers attracted to the unusual events on the Common. Despite Conway Jenkins' insistence that the lane should be closed, it remained open, and the problem was only solved after the introduction of bye-laws which restricted its use to holders of permits which were issued to bona fide users of Hayes Lane, on application.†

The disadvantages of having what almost amounted to an aircraft factory thrust upon them soon became apparent to local residents. They complained about the noise, not only from the aeroplanes but also from the heavy lorries that ran a shuttle service to railway stations transporting aeroplane parts. There were also complaints about the constant whirring of aero-engines as they were run up on test; in fact Joe Hoare, who was farming Waterhouse Farm, suggested that the noise was turning his cows' milk sour.

It is worth bearing in mind that Kenley was a quiet rural district which had seen little change in centuries; to have had the tranquillity of the area so dramatically shattered by an industry which has never been known for its quietness must have been an unsettling experience. These unfortunate circumstances were further extended by the noise created by building contractors' lorries as they supplied materials to a site on the other side of Hayes Lane where seven large permanent Belfast-type aeroplane sheds and ancillary buildings were being constructed for aeroplane storage and workshops.

To their credit, R.F.C. personnel soon established themselves locally as a fine sporting bunch, excelling at soccer, with several league players in

*The Bessonneaux hangar was the standard portable hangar of the R.F.C., and was virtually a tent. It had a buttressed wooden frame over which a heavy canvas cover was stretched, and it could provide shelter for five or six of the smaller types of aeroplane. Those who knew them will remember that, when entering one, the magically evocative smell of burnt castor oil and aviation spirit hung in the air and was exuded from the very fabric of the building.

†See Appendix one.

Progress with the building of the sheds, 1917. Hayes Lane can be seen at top left.
Air Chief Marshal Sir Leslie Hollinghurst

the team. Flight Lieutenant "Bill" Adams was the prime mover in the sporting world and managed the successful team which won the King's Cup in the Cross Country Championships in January, 1919. From their ranks also came a number of talented entertainers who formed the "Kenley Kommon Koncert Party" which gave performances in local halls and did a good deal of charity work among the community. Dai Jenkins, a professional singer, actor and writer, was the great inspiration behind the group, doing most of the organisation.

H. M. Reay, M.B.E., who was a corporal clerk and stenographer with the R.F.C., writes of the early days:

The Canadian Forestry Corps spent several weeks clearing the land and were billeted in private houses in the Kenley area while doing the job. On completion, the aerodrome, or to give it the correct name, No. 7 Kenley Aircraft Acceptance Park, came into existence.

Naturally it started in a small way. We lived under canvas, with a marquee for the dining hall and another for the Canteen and Y.M.C.A. All of the assembly workshops and aeroplanes were housed in the Bessonneaux hangars.

As autumn approached, building work on the permanent sheds, workshops and offices made steady progress and, knowing that winter was just around the corner, N.C.O.s and men were being accommodated in large empty houses in the surrounding district such as "Whyteleafe House" at the bottom of Whyteleafe Hill and "Lovell" at Kenley. The Officers' Mess was in "The Garth" down Welcomes Road.

By 1918 barrack rooms were built and the aerodrome had become one vast self-contained unit, collecting and receiving parts of aeroplanes from factories spread far and wide; these we built into fighting aeroplanes complete with engines and guns and then, when fully tested,* they were transferred to France ready for action. The usual procedure was to fly them down to Lympne near Folkestone and then on over the English Channel to France. Occasionally one would come adrift en route to the coast and the pilot had to phone in and ask us to send down a Crossley Tender to pick it up from where he had forced landed.

The work force developed until it consisted of several hundred aircraftsmen including riggers, fitters, armourers, clerical staff and a complement of aerial gunners and pilots. This unit did not just grow overnight; 1917–18 were the really vital years. There were many comings and goings from the railway stations of Upper Warlingham, Whyteleafe and Kenley, which were kept exceedingly busy as they dealt not only with us but also with normal "goods" and passenger traffic. The genial stationmaster at Upper Warlingham, George Byard, also had to cater for the Guards Depot at Caterham and an infantry camp. The heavy Leyland lorries that we used to transport the crated aeroplane components from the stations stood out on the aerodrome all night and, if it had been cold, the starting up of their big engines was quite a business; in those days they all had to be started on the handle.

The guiding hand in the first instance was the Commanding Officer, Major Thom. He was followed by Major McCallum, a production specialist, who directed and obtained maximum production in the shortest possible time. Under his control a first-class, efficient unit emerged. The welfare of officers and men was not

---

*Occasionally a square of white canvas was spread on the ground to the North of Riddlesdown railway tunnel and aircraft dived down and used it for target practice.

overlooked, but aeroplane production was first priority and he saw to this. I think we were producing S.E.5s, Sopwith Dolphins and Camels at the time. In his office the walls were painted and set out to show the movement of aeroplanes from hangar to hangar, as the rigging was completed, engines installed, guns mounted and tested and so on. People from the hangars phoned in hourly and, as the clerks chalked up the information, he could tell at a glance the situation of all planes and what stage they were at. His "wall pictures" also included the numbers of officers and men and their general trades, capacities, and physical categories. The movements in and out were frequent and the Air Ministry, at the Hotel Cecil in the Strand, kept close tabs on all figures, insisting that every night a motor-cyclist should bring information on aeroplanes, personnel, etc., to them.

The testing of machines was constant. It follows that there were a number of accidents, but generally a high standard was maintained. The purr of the engines, especially on a Sunday morning, was a sound welcomed by all those responsible for keeping the Front Line supplied.

One morning in 1917 was memorable. The machine of Lieutenant Courey, V.C., crashed on the 'drome and caught fire. About a dozen men dashed to his aid and Sergeant Woodward, having used his fire extinguisher, dashed in and hauled him out. He was badly burned and injured, but made a remarkable recovery in hospital. Sergeant Woodward was awarded the M.S.M. for his part in the rescue and this was presented to him by Brigadier-General Jenkins on the aerodrome. When he had recovered, Courey returned and shook hands with all of us who had assisted in his

A Sopwith Camel received as part of a batch of three hundred from T. O. M. Sopwith's factory at Kingston, Surrey. Having been tested by Lieutenant Hollinghurst, it went on to serve with No 45 Squadron.   *Lieutenant-Colonel F. A. G. Noel*

rescue. Brigadier-General Conway Jenkins often came at weekends and flew his own special B.E.2C, which he kept on the aerodrome.*

After America had declared war on Germany, one of their Air Force units came to train as mechanics. What I remember most about them was the day they complained about the food. During the summer it was very warm and we were given Australian rabbits to eat. (You could smell the rabbits before you even got near them.) The Americans refused to eat them and the whole lot of them went on strike for the rest of the day. The British people didn't. We took them in our stride, we were so hungry. We didn't get an awful lot to eat. Tea was usually hard biscuits and a bit of jam.

Fog was one of our troubles. It descended quickly and was so thick that, when it was time to leave in the evening, occasionally it was impossible to get off the aerodrome. In these conditions, finding the stile to the path which allowed me to take the short cut down to the road was very difficult. Whyteleafe Road hill in those days was completely unlit and, with no houses except the old almshouses at the bottom, the fog had the effect of making the journey quite eerie.

The disciplinarian of the camp was Sergeant-Major Woods (Timber Woods), an ex-Guards N.C.O. and regular soldier, who had been wounded at Mons in 1914. His voice carried almost as far as the Guards Depot at Caterham (nearly a mile). I remember that one ex-infantryman was very short in stature but had somehow been issued with a coat that was so long that it nearly touched the ground. Seeing him on parade, Timber Woods addressed him in the grand style: "Where the hell have you come from, the b----y cavalry?" It must surely have been heard by every living creature within a radius of half a mile. He was everything a good sergeant-major should be, and we respected him for it.

The aerodrome was guarded by Boer War veterans; men of the Royal Defence Corps. If ever you arrived back late at night without a midnight pass, it was the accepted thing to cross their palm with silver in the form of a silver threepenny piece; I always made sure that I carried a small number with me.

Women were recruited locally to supplement the few full-time members of the W.R.A.F. who were supervised by Mrs Callard, wife of one of the officers. Two of the W.R.A.F. girls were dispatch riders, and each had a motor-cycle combination. After a spell of rainy weather, the large holes in the surface of the local roads filled with water, and the girls gained much enjoyment by dipping their unfortunate sidecar passengers in and out of the holes as they rode along. Once I was a victim and arrived at the Commanding Officer's door covered in mud after having been systematically dunked in and out of very nearly every pot-hole en route. "Just look at the state of me," I said to the girl. "Don't worry, you'll do," she laughingly replied.

One night we heard the drone of the engines of a raider as it passed overhead, and a pilot and his gunner rushed to an aeroplane and climbed in before realising the complete futility of their action. The situation was impossible; they were in no way equipped for night fighting; nor had they the power to get up there quickly.

One of the most famous aeroplane types that passed through the Kenley park was the Sopwith Camel, of which nearly three hundred were received from T. O. M. Sopwith's factory at Kingston. Later these were superseded by the Sopwith Dolphin, a faster multi-gunned aeroplane. The Camel gained a certain notoriety as being a difficult and often vicious aeroplane to fly, and a number of inexperienced pilots were to

*Conway Jenkins often flew himself to aerodromes in his charge, including those in France.

A B.E.2c used by General L. E. O. Charlton, D.S.O. *Lieutenant-Colonel F. A. G. Noel*

The Station Commander and Captain A. J. "Bill" Adams with the Station cross-country running team of 1919.

give their lives to its idiosyncrasies. In the hands of the expert, however, it was a highly manoeuvrable machine and a formidable opponent in the sky over France.

To try to allay the fears associated with it and to improve its image, Captain D. V. Armstrong of No 151 Squadron gave flying exhibitions at some aerodromes, including Kenley. His mastery of low-level aerobatics earned him a reputation as one of the finest and most daring pilots in the country, and it is said that he once rolled a Camel so low down that its wingtips brushed the top of the long grass. Two weeks before the end of the war he misjudged a spin while "stunting" in France and was killed, sometimes the fate of those who have an inner driving force which compels them to exercise regularly their great skill and the capability of their machine to the utmost. Captain H. W. Woollett, of No 43 Squadron, was also a fine exponent of the machine. An outstandingly successful day for him was 12th April, 1918, when he shot down six enemy aircraft. His final score of victories in the war amounted to thirty-five.

During 1918 several bomber squadrons were mobilised, No 88 Squadron departing in April and No 108 Squadron, under the command

"The Garth" in Welcomes Road, Kenley, which was used as the Officers' Mess in 1917.   *Author*

of South African Major S. S. Halse, leaving in D.H.9s for Cappelle on 18th July after receiving a farewell visit from Mr Bonar Law and several other members of the War Cabinet. At the end of the following month, No 110 (Bomber) Squadron left in the new Liberty engined 'A' version of the D.H.9, bound for Courban Depot and then on to the forward base at Bettancourt, its Commanding Officer, Major H. R. Nicholl, having in his charge a complete squadron of aeroplanes which had been presented to the R.F.C. by his Serene Highness The Nizam of Hyderabad.* This was probably the last completely new squadron to go to France. Unfortunately their losses were soon severe; in only three raids on Germany between 16th September and 5th October, ten of their number were lost; several others came to grief almost immediately. In no time at all the squadron's losses, including non-combatant mishaps, were catastrophic.†

When the Armistice was declared at 11 a.m. on 11th November, 1918, Major McCallum announced the news to a full parade, assembled on the aerodrome, ending with the words, "There is free beer in the Canteen." Later, a triumphant march, led by an American band, left Kenley and wound its way down the hill and on to Croydon.

All construction work on the seven large permanent sheds (erected by Minters and a Southampton contractor, Baker) was completed and they were in use by the end of the war. At the end of 1918 efforts were being concentrated on one very large shed on the western side of Hayes Lane specifically designed for Handley Page and Vickers Vimy long-range bombers, which were about to come into service. Although some doubted the advisability of the building, particularly with regard to its siting on the other side of Hayes Lane, which would involve difficulty of access to the field over the public thoroughfare, it was completed the following year.

Kenley's primary role as an Aircraft Acceptance Park was soon to finish, allowing local railway stations to return to their peacetime way of life and giving the local lanes freedom from heavy lorries and their appendages. Occasionally aeroplanes had arrived from the railway station with the wings on the back of a lorry and the fuselage being towed backwards on its wheels, hitched behind the lorry. The greatest contribution to the war effort had been in stockpiling and preparing aeroplanes for the squadrons in France, and any assistance in the air

*One of these aeroplanes is now preserved in the Bomber Command Museum, Hendon. It had been lost on the 5th October raid in 1917. The machine could not have been very badly damaged when arriving on German soil. Having survived the Second World War in Berlin, it turned up in Poland and was eventually exchanged by a museum in Krakow for one of the R.A.F. Museum's Spitfires.

†Some time later, an American pilot leaving in a similar machine was killed when it crashed on the railway line near to the entrance of Riddlesdown tunnel. A further catastrophe was avoided by a signalman waving a red flag rushing to stop the Eastbourne express.

A D.H.9A of No 110 Squadron now preserved in the R.A.F. Museum, Hendon. This machine, serial number F.1010, was received from Westlands and proceeded overseas on 31st August, 1918, landing at Lympne, Le Bourget, and Courban, arriving at Bettancourt on 1st September. Flown on operations by Captain Andrew Glover Inglis, it was one of three aircraft lost on a raid on Kaiserslautern and Pirmasens on 5th October, 1918. *Author*

defence of London was negligible, if not non-existent. The prime justification for the aerodrome's existence had been fulfilled.

In a report dated 16th July, 1917, advising the setting up of a "Directorate of Aircraft Acceptance", Lieutenant-Colonel Conway Jenkins stated that at that time all the Aircraft Acceptance Parks in the country were receiving three hundred machines a month from various sources: he anticipated that by early Summer the following year (1918) this number would increase to 4,500 machines per month. Whether this figure was ever achieved is difficult to ascertain; it could well be that he was overstating his case.

Before the park expired, communications flying throughout Europe was being operated on a large scale by 86 (Communications) Wing, with No 1 Squadron which had been formed earlier at Hendon and No 2 Squadron based at Buc, near Paris. Flights to Brussels, Hesdin and Marquise interspersed their main occupation, which was the regular transportation of despatches, mail and persons involved in the Paris Peace Conference being held at Versailles. For this purpose on average two Martinsyde Scouts, twenty de Havilland 4As and eight Handley Page 0/400s (the large, heavy bombers) were kept in commission; some of the latter were converted to carry passengers. Three of these were given a less military appearance by being decorated in an overall silver finish. With suitably luxurious internal fittings (at least one sported a small cocktail cabinet) and a name, *Silver Star, Prince of Wales, Great Britain*, each with the prefix H.M.A.L. (His Majesty's Air Liner), a less warlike image was nurtured. Even so, their origins were still visibly obvious. To the V.I.P.s and delegates the ferrying service provided a reasonably comfortable and comparatively quick means of transport to Buc and

A D.H.4A of No 2 (Communications) Squadron, used mainly in the regular transportation of despatches between Britain and the Paris Peace Conference held at Versailles.
Science Museum, London

The Officers of No 7 (Kenley) Aircraft Acceptance Park in December, 1917. Back row: Lieutenants Dodge, Hazelgrove, Heard, Hollinghurst, Smith, Selwyn and Cardwell. Middle row: Lieutenants Bell, Hall, Hurley, Sutton, Watts, Williams, Lyon, Mudge and Nicholl. Front row, sitting: Captain Wall, R.A.M.C., Captain Orde, Captain Morris, M.C., Major Thom, M.C., Captain Livingston, M.C., Captain Patteson, M.C., and Lieutenant Wilson. *Lieutenant-Colonel F. A G. Noel*

back, averaging two hours thirty-eight minutes each way, the flying time depending largely on prevailing winds and weather conditions.

By the end of July, 1919, the squadrons had flown 3,500 hours, carrying 670 passengers and 750 mail bags, plus urgent despatches carried by the smaller Martinsydes. The Wing also contributed a substantial amount of domestic flying, and leaflets advertising the Victory Loan were dropped over London and other cities by No 1 Squadron.

The Peace Conference flights were not without incident; a D.H.4 transporting Major-General Sykes crashed on the aerodrome soon after taking off, killing the pilot, Captain Edward Middleton Knott. At the inquest held in the *Rose and Crown* public house at Riddlesdown the cause of the accident was given as engine failure, the reason being that a mechanic had neglected to fill the radiator, causing the engine to overheat and seize up. The pilot had neither sufficient speed nor height to manoeuvre, and it left him in an impossible situation which cost him his life. Crashes in bad weather caused two more fatalities.

Another incident, a near tragedy which fortunately had a happy ending and probably became the source of much badinage in the Mess

17

for weeks afterwards, is recalled by Air Commodore W. H. Primrose, C.B.E., D.F.C., who as a lieutenant-colonel and later wing commander commanded No 86 (Communications) Wing.

On the first night service between Kenley and Buc, we carried as a member of the crew a chap who must have been a progenitor of Percy Prune (Bill Hooper's notorious cartoon character). He left the emergency hatch in the floor of the Handley Page open and, in putting on his "Mae West",* accidentally inflated the garment. Going up forward to ask the pilot what he should do about it, he fell through the open hatch but was prevented by his blown-up "Mae West" from reaching the Channel. No one was aware of his plight, on which he was able to meditate for the rest of the journey, while he became exceedingly cold from the waist downwards. The moral seems to be that if you are going to survive as a clot you've got to be a proper clot.

One of the Wing's most celebrated flights took place on 21st June, 1919, when Canadian Lieutenants Yates and Vance, accompanied by Mechanics Stedman and Hand, flew a V.I.P. to Cairo in a Handley Page 0/400 (F.318). They reached Cairo in five days after a whole chapter of accidents and incidents, the actual time in the air being only thirty-six hours.

At this time Air Vice-Marshal R. P. Willock was also at Kenley, and he recalls:

My first experience of Kenley was when I was O.C. No. 1 (Communications) Squadron in 1918 when Wing Commander (Air Commodore Retired) W. H. Primrose, D.F.C., was commanding the Communications Wing. The Squadron was established to provide communications between London and Paris for the Peace Conference, and we had some very distinguished V.I.P.s, including Winston Churchill, travelling between the two capitals. McCrindle, who later became Managing Director (External Affairs) B.O.A.C., was in command of No. 2 (Communications) Squadron which was stationed at Buc, Paris, and the two squadrons ran parallel services. I remember carrying out the first night flight between Kenley and Paris in a Handley Page 0/400 with Chadwick as pilot, which in those days was quite an event. Furthermore, the two communications squadrons were, of course, the forerunners of civil aviation as we know it today.

If I remember rightly, I was C.O. of the Station on the first occasion in 1919 when it was a Stores Park. It was during a period of demobilisation after the First World War and Royal Air Force strength was being reduced daily. The hangars were chock-a-block with aircraft standing perpendicularly to save space, leaving insufficient room to walk through them, much less maintain the aircraft. We also had a shortage of personnel. I had only been in command a comparatively short period when I was informed that Sir John Salmond would inspect the Station.

After endeavouring to walk through the first hangar he said, "I have seen quite enough of this, take me to your office", where he sat in my chair and told me that it was the worst Station he had ever inspected. A remark with which, foolishly perhaps, I heartily agreed. "Stuffy" Dowding was there at the time and kindly stood by me and said to Sir John, "Willock reminds me of a Battery R.A. Commander of mine who,

*The current inflatable life jacket in use at the time. It was not known as a "Mae West" until later.

18

Captain A. J. "Bill" Adams with the Kenley mixed hockey team, 1919.

when his Battery was being inspected, was told by the Inspecting Officer that it was the worst body of men he had ever inspected. To which the Battery Commander replied, 'Wait until you have seen the rear rank, Sir!'" However, I managed to live down that inspection and was subsequently posted to Manston.

While steps were being taken by the Royal Air Force to dispose of the enormous surplus of aeroplanes and spares which had been accumulated during the war, twelve local lads from Whyteleafe were doing their best to ease the situation at Kenley. When they appeared before the Croydon County Bench they were accused of stealing twenty-two wheels, tyres, covers, axles (8–10 feet long) and a number of various other aeroplane parts to the value of £15 from the Kenley "unserviceable dump". It appears from the evidence that this was not just an isolated incident. One of the parents remarked "There are dozens of these wheels and axles in use on barrows and trucks in the village. Seeing grown-up people

19

wheeling them about, I naturally thought that they were being given away at the aerodrome."

In just a few years the rapid advance of aviation technology made it possible to manufacture aeroplanes of sufficient size and power to enable a number of passengers to be transported and the idea of carrying them on a commercial basis was a natural progression. In France, Henri Farman prepared one of his large twin-engined F60 "Goliath" machines for a trip from Paris to London, but after receiving the go-ahead from the French authorities he was baulked by their British counterparts. The reason for the objection was that the flight could not be classified as a military operation and restrictions on civilian flying were still in force. Farman persevered, however, and cunningly persuaded the French Government to buy the machine; he then filled it with thirteen military personnel and, under the pilotage of Lieutenant Bossoutrot, flew it from Toussus-le-Noble to Kenley on 8th February, 1919. The purpose of the flight by the F60 "Aerobus" is somewhat obscure; it can really only be regarded as an attempt to gain prestige prior to the possible introduction of commercial air services, as the aeroplane's name implied. The same machine left Paris three days later on a similar journey to Brussels and on this occasion Mr and Mrs Henri Farman were among the passengers. By September, French aeroplanes were flying to Hounslow, and the following year Farman "Goliaths" became a common sight in the sky over Southern England as they operated regularly on the London–Paris route into Croydon.

CHAPTER TWO

Years of Peace

A T THE END of the war the need for military aerodromes naturally diminished and it therefore surprised some people to see that development at Kenley continued. Local residents watched and noted that the aerodrome was taking on an even greater air of permanency. What of the future? They organised a petition and pressed for questions to be asked in the House. Their worst fears were justified. In a written reply in December to a question by Sir Stuart Coates, Mr Winston Churchill said that a large amount of money had already been spent on the aerodrome, that its situation rendered it of great importance in connection with the future air defence of London, and it was considered desirable that it should be retained as a permanent R.A.F. station. He was, incidentally, quietly receiving flying lessons at the aerodrome.

Although the R.A.F. had established themselves with some conviction on the site, none of it actually belonged to them and they spent the next two and a half years looking at their legal position and seeking approval from the Treasury for its purchase. Eventually, happy in the knowledge that the Defence of the Realm Act would enable them to proceed with the purchase in spite of any objections which were likely to be raised, they opened negotiations with those concerned. By far the largest obstacle to be overcome was the acquisition of the Common, a piece of which (approximately one-fifth) they decided to return for public use. As compensation for retaining the larger part, the Air Council offered to purchase land overlooking Whyteleafe on the north-east boundary as a substitute. An agreement was eventually made with the City of London on 17th November, 1921, which finally became an Act in August, 1922. One of the conditions incorporated was that Hayes Lane should stay open for public use. The old problem remained; aeroplanes occupying the large shed on the western side of the lane had to cross it in order to get to the field, an undesirable and hazardous business for both pilots and travellers on the road. This somewhat ridiculous state of affairs remained until the shed was demolished in 1936, and it was not until just before the beginning of the Second World War in 1939 that a decision to divert the lane was finally made. Other conditions enshrined in the Act were that no building should be erected on the land that was once Kenley

Common and that this land would revert to the City of London if ever the R.A.F. no longer needed the aerodrome.

While negotiations were in abeyance pending the purchase of the substitute land, the Air Council involved itself in obtaining the rest of the aerodrome site, the bulk of which came to them in a 120-acre deal with Joseph Sawyer and Another on 22nd December, 1921. Flintfield House and land had been acquired in 1918 and was bought in 1920.

During 1920 the aerodrome took on a new importance when it became the home of No 1 Group, Inland Area, commanded (in the days when a group captain really did command a group) by Group Captain H. C. T. Dowding, C.M.G., who later distinguished himself as the leader of Fighter Command during the Battle of Britain. He writes:

> I don't happen to remember the incident which Willock related,* but I expect it is correct. Anyway, that was a story about a notorious Gunner Major which was current when I was a subaltern.
>
> I do remember some other stories of inspecting officers, but they are not very kindly ones, nor perhaps calculated to stimulate recruiting. It might perhaps be of interest, however, to recall the "relay race" which was always such a feature of the

*See page 18.

Opposite: "Flintfield House," taken over under the Defence of the Realm Act in 1917 and used as offices and Mess. It was demolished in October, 1980.
Author

Right: The internal wooden structure of a hangar of 1917 vintage.
Author

early Pageants at Hendon. I remember that an Avro started from rest and flew a circuit and the pilot handed over his baton to a Bristol pilot, who handed it over in turn to the pilot of a Snipe for a third lap. I remember pointing out to Robb, who was then a flight lieutenant, that practically the whole thing depended on starting the Avro at the first swing of the prop when it had a semi-warmed engine that had been stopped for ten minutes after taxi-ing out 300 yards to the start. Robb organised some extensive practice on these lines, with the result that Kenley won the relay race (I think) three years running.

The Flight Lieutenant Robb to whom Lord Dowding refers went on to become Air Chief Marshal Sir James Robb, G.C.B., K.B.E., D.S.O., D.F.C., A.F.C., a truly great name in R.A.F. history. Extracts from his log book, coupled with his personal comments, give some indication of what was required of a service pilot at this time.

E. H. Johnston was commanding 24 Squadron the whole time I was in it and he followed me to Iraq before the end of 1922. The others of the permanent team were Luxmoore, R. W. Chappell, Augustus Bird, N. H. Jenkins (killed on a long-distance record attempt) and that remarkable character Trapagna Leroy. The last-named was the finest De Havilland 9A pilot in the country and did a phenomenal amount of flying and instruction on this type, before one day an engine finally packed up low down over Purley.

Captain J. M. Robb — Northumberland Fusiliers and R.A.F.

Extracts from log books

Formed "Air Council Inspection Squadron" at Croydon, 24th Sept., 1919, after bringing home from Germany the personnel of 92 Squadron (92 was commanded by Major Arthur Coningham and I had taken the personnel to France as senior Flight Commander when the Squadron went overseas in June, 1918).

A.C.I.S. was commanded by Squadron Leader E. H. Johnston, C.B.C., late of 20 Squadron, title changed to "24" when we moved to Kenley in January, 1920.

24.9.19	Test of new S.E.5A (Fitted with a parachute).
29.9.19	Bringing Sopwith Triplane from Waddon.
1.10.19	Croydon to Kenley in D.H.9 (General Seely's) attached to No 1 Comm. Sqdn., Kenley, for Strike Duty. Delivering mails during the Railway Strike. Rejoined A.C.I.S. 7.10.19.
13.10.19	First flight in Martinsyde F.4 (Rolls R. engine).
20.10.19	Delivered rat-traps to four airfields in Kent. Rat invasion at its height!
21.11.19	Testing a three-seater D.H.4A.
28.11.19	To Kenley in Bristol Fighter to inspect quarters.
7.1.20	*Start of move to Kenley* (In D.H.4).
30.1.20	Testing Col. Ludlow-Hewitt's Bristol.
5.2.20	Special Flight to Paris at C.A.S. request to collect despatches. In Bristol Tourer.
12.2.20	Start of delivery to Ireland of Group Capt. Bonham-Carter's special Be2C, fitted with rudder control on joy-stick. Landed Coventry en route for Shotwick for petrol.
16.2.20	Held up at Shotwick until 16th owing to weather. Crossed to Baldonnel on this day in 2 hours 30 mins. Good trip in spite of bad weather. Waller and two other Bristol pilots who had waited about a fortnight before attempting the crossing, took off on the same day. All three aircraft were never seen again.
31.3.20	In Bristol Fighter, took up F/O Pitcher for Wireless Telephony experiments. They were "dud"!
22.4.20	Delivering a Bristol Fr. to Eastchurch. Brought back by F/O Alex Coryton.
10.5.20	To Farnborough. Collected a D.H.9R. First flight in D.H.9 modified to be fitted with the new Napier Lion engine. Aircraft to be kept for C.A.S. (Air Marshal Trenchard).
4.6.20	In 1404, my favourite of the 24 Bristols in the flight. To Frinton to inspect the proposed civil airfield. Forced landing owing to oil tank shortage. Bought some Castrol at a garage and flew back to Kenley.
8.6.20	Start of formation flying practice for the first R.A.F. Pageant at Hendon.
18.6.20	Taking G/Capt. Ludlow-Hewitt's special Bristol to Duxford. On return flight in another Bristol with F/O F. L. Luxmoore, had three forced landings. First in a field near Saffron Walden, second and third on Naval airfield at Chingford. Return to Kenley by train.
3.7.20	The first Aerial Pageant at Hendon. 24 Squadron took part in three events on Bristols and won the Avro and the three type race.
23.7.20	First flight in a D.H.9A—Liberty engine, passenger F/O A. Coryton— Delivering to Gosport.

20.9.20	First flight of the LE PERC—a two seater fighter. 400 H.P. Liberty engine—built in U.S.A. and assembled by my flight for U.S. Air Attaché. I took him up six days later—about the only occasion on which he flew in it!
21.2.21	My flight was used for refresher and occasional "ab initio" training. On this date two of the "refreshers" tested were F/Lt. C. N. Lowe, who required no dual, and F/Lt. Beauchamp-Proctor. Latter first back to flying duties after completing his university training in South Africa.
16.5.21	Visit of Crown Prince of Japan [now Emperor Hirohito] to 24 Squadron. Gave demonstration in Vimy, then took part in formation flying. Final event was a flight for one of the Senior Japanese generals in the back of a Bristol. Got told off for looping him!
10.6.21	In middle of intensive flying practices for the second Pageant. Secretary of State for Air (F. E. Guest) taken to visit the airfields on Salisbury Plain. I had Group Captain A. F. L. Scott as my passenger.
2.7.21	2nd Pageant at Hendon. Took part in Formation Flying. Heat and final of Relay Race, Bombing Village. Ruined the Queen's white kid gloves when presented to her in the Royal Enclosure, by having to come straight from Bristol with oily hands!
10.8.21	Visit of Emir of Katsina whom I had to receive and show 24 Squadron to. Solved difficulty by taking him and his son into the air.
11.7.21	Lent one of the Bristols to Traill of Biggin Hill, he crashed it. Air Vice Marshal T. S. Traill, who helped us out on many occasions, especially when 24 could not raise the full number of 9 pilots for the Pageant formations.
28.8.21	Taking off in D.H.9A the crankshaft broke at 50 feet. Piled up on Coulsdon Common. The 10th forced landing to date (two bad) in 24 Squadron but the only one in which the aircraft was wrecked.
23.9.21	Refresher passenger—Flight Lieutenant S. M. Kinkead.
15.6.21	Visit of Inspection by S. of S. for Air (Captain F. E. Guest) to Cranwell, Martlesham, Howden. Group Captain A. F. L. Scott was F/O. Luxmoore's passenger in D.H.9As.
15.9.21	Taking S. of S. to Paris for Conference. Weather very thick.
20.9.21	Return flight, solo. S. of S. unable to wait for weather clearance. Just as well as engine of Bristol stopped when over mid-Channel above cloud layer, at 6,000 feet. Landed in sea off Folkestone and Bristol sank in 12 minutes. Was picked up without much delay, thanks to prompt action by F/O. C. A. B. Wilcock who lived in flat on sea front.
20.6.22	3rd Aerial Pageant. 24 took part in or organised the same events as last year. Relay race won for 3rd year running, the team

R. W. Chappell — Avro
J. M. Robb — Bristol
F. L. Luxmoore — Snipe

9.8.22	Landing a Bristol in front of hangar at Northolt, ran into and killed three sheep. Could not be seen owing to the length of the grass.

Total hours flying with 24 Squadron—570 hours.

Approx. number of purely instructional flights—630.

As can be seen, although aviation had advanced considerably, aero-engines were still prone to the occasional failure, and your future depended largely on an element of luck as to just where you were when this occurred.

The year 1923 marked the end of the "rundown" after the First World War and a small seed of expansion began to germinate. This included the building up of the Home Defence Force. Fighter squadrons of First World War vintage were re-formed; one of them, No 32, which was eventually equipped with Sopwith Snipes and commanded by Squadron Leader T. E. B. Howe, A.F.C., made its home at Kenley. Surprisingly, so soon after the glut left over from the war, the squadron was short of aeroplanes and by the end of the year its strength was made up of only three Snipes and two Avros; the other Snipes were still in the process of manufacture. This was the sum total of equipment when C. W. A. Scott joined the squadron in December, fresh and green from Flying Training School. Anxious to show his prowess, he obtained permission to fly one of the coveted Snipes; he immediately took off, performed a number of outrageous aerobatics, stalled it at thirty feet and crashed, leaving the machine a total wreck. Several years later he achieved lasting fame for his long-distance record-breaking flights between Britain and Australia.

While the squadron was working up, the aerodrome's importance was further emphasised when it became the headquarters of the newly formed No 6 Group, which was responsible for the control of all fighter squadrons involved in the protection of the homeland. It was put under the command of the formidable Air Commodore C. R. Samson. All the squadrons were based in the southern part of the country; No 56 at Biggin Hill, No 41 at Northolt, Nos 25 and 17 at Hawkinge and No 32 taking pride of place as home squadron. To help him maintain a close watch on his command, Samson ordered a Siskin for his personal use, and it was ferried in from Farnborough by a young pilot officer who was destined to play a leading role in the history of the Station and the R.A.F., Theodore McEvoy of 41 Squadron, later Air Chief Marshal Sir Theodore McEvoy. The arrival of the all-white Siskin J.7171 on any aerodrome thereafter was always greeted with some trepidation, all the more so when it arrived unannounced, for Samson gained a reputation for occasionally sending a signal to one station advising them that he was about to visit them and then, when the word had been passed around on the grapevine of his intentions, he arrived out of the blue at some other unsuspecting station, just to keep people on their toes.

In the main, life was carefree and easy. Flying, particularly during the twenties, was distinguished more for its enjoyable aspects than anything else. Great rivalry developed between squadrons as the pilots attempted to out-fly each other, often leading to hilarious results for the participants. The airmen's exploits were received less enthusiastically by those in authority. Air Commodore D'Arcy Greig, D.F.C., A.F.C., a member of the successful team which won the Schneider Trophy for Britain in 1929, was then a flight commander in 24 Squadron. He tells of one such incident which grew to such proportions that it became known as the Kenley–Northolt War:

Hostilities broke out as the result of the following incident. Immediately after lunch one very murky afternoon in late January or early February, 1924, we had packed up flying for the day as it was only just possible to see the trees on the northern boundary of the airfield, when viewed from the tarmac. We had all settled down comfortably in the warmth of our respective Flight Offices when we heard the roar of approaching aircraft, and a few seconds later nine Northolt Siskins emerged from the mist, flying at nought feet and obviously conducting themselves in what we took to be a most scornful manner. Justly incensed by this obvious slight on the honour of 24 Squadron, we held an immediate conference and it was decided that I should approach the C.O., Squadron Leader R. S. Maxwell, M.C., D.F.C., with the suggestion that a "Bumf Raid" should immediately be carried out on Northolt. Immediate approval was granted, and while the aircraft and pilots were being detailed, a chap called Alford and myself drove down to Caterham where we visited a number of chemist's shops and bought as many toilet rolls as they could spare.

When we arrived back at the airfield, sixteen aircraft were ready to take off, a very odd assortment of Avro 504K, DH9A, Bristol Fighter, Snipe, and three Fawns. The "bumf" was quickly distributed, and the aircraft took off at rough intervals,

The visit of the Japanese Crown Prince on 16th May, 1921, when large crowds were present to watch pilots of No 24 Squadron display a variety of aircraft. Air Vice-Marshal Sir John Salmond, accompanying the inspecting officer, is followed by Flight Lieutenant J. M. Robb.
Air Chief Marshal Sir James Robb

according to type and performance. By this time it was getting late and the visibility was lousy. However, by the greatest of luck we all arrived over Northolt at the same time and we fairly plastered the place. On the run up to the target the Mono engine of Bowen-Buscarlet's aircraft packed up. He consequently had to force-land on Northolt Airfield and was promptly taken prisoner. After the last of the hostile aircraft had set course for base, he was taken under escort and made to clear up the mess, on completion of which he was suitably entertained for the rest of that day and repatriated the following morning.

Some days later, a reprisal raid was carried out by Northolt, and a highly lethal load of boots (unserviceable, various) was scattered over Kenley. The effect of this raid was devastating, and for a while 24 Squadron was at a loss as to what to do next. However, a day or two later a party visited a well-known and very exclusive club at 43 Gerrard Street and, in the early hours of the following morning, when driving homeward down Jermyn Street (why, I do not know—perhaps the guiding hand of providence) a couple of quite large and very ornamental trees mounted in green wooden tubs were spotted outside the entrance of some hotel. It was at once realised that these were just what Northolt wanted, so they were quickly loaded into the back of one of the cars (all ancient open types).

The following day, the trees were securely loaded into the back of two Bristol Fighters which were flown with a powerful escort to Northolt. While the escort beat

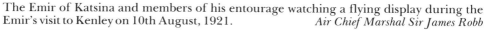

The Emir of Katsina and members of his entourage watching a flying display during the Emir's visit to Kenley on 10th August, 1921. *Air Chief Marshal Sir James Robb*

Bristol Fighters of No 24 Squadron practising for the R.A.F. Pageant in July, 1921, with Riddlesdown Quarry in the background. The unusual aircraft nearest the camera is a Bristol "Tourer".   *Air Chief Marshal Sir James Robb*

up the hangars and tarmac, the Bristols were landed and the trees planted in the circle.

Northolt did not retaliate, and arrangements had just been completed by Kenley for a further raid in which a number of stray dogs and cats were to be landed on Northolt Airfield when Air Commodore C. R. Samson decided that perhaps things had gone far enough, so an armistice was arranged.

While doing a spinning test in a Gamecock, after twenty-seven turns and a height loss of six thousand feet the aircraft became uncontrollable, forcing D'Arcy Greig to take to his parachute. The aircraft continued in its right-handed spin until crashing two miles away. The turns in the Spithead Schneider Trophy course two years later were less severe but taken at a far greater speed, and it was flying the beautiful Supermarine S.6 seaplane that was one of the highlights of his career.

In May, 1926, No 6 Group became "Fighting Area" under a new command known as Air Defence of Great Britain. Soon after the change,

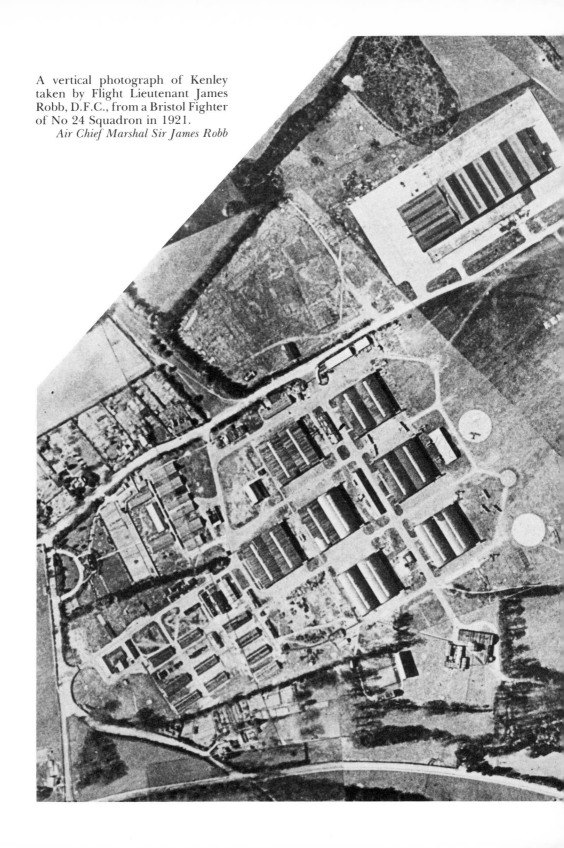

A vertical photograph of Kenley taken by Flight Lieutenant James Robb, D.F.C., from a Bristol Fighter of No 24 Squadron in 1921.
Air Chief Marshal Sir James Robb

Air Vice-Marshal H. R. M. Brooke-Popham, C.B., C.M.G., D.S.O., A.F.C., took over the Group, remaining at Kenley for a short time before moving his headquarters to Uxbridge, where it later became No 11 Group.

Air Chief Marshal Sir Robert Brooke-Popham recalls the contribution of the Kenley squadrons during the 1926 General Strike:

> On the outbreak of the General Strike, I was about to join up as a stoker on a railway locomotive when I was called into the Air Ministry to organise an air communication service throughout Great Britain for official letters and the official newspaper, the *British Gazette*. The squadrons at Kenley, I think, 24 and 32, were used almost exclusively for this purpose. Air Commodore Samson was then still commanding No 6 Group with Headquarters at Kenley and under the stimulus of his drive and example the air mail service continued to operate successfully even in bad weather and often with heavy loads of mail and papers, and gained the admiration and gratitude of Whitehall.
>
> A few days after the strike was over I arrived at Kenley by air from Andover to take over No 6 Group from Samson and to form "Fighting Area", so it is right to say that Fighting Area, and so Fighter Command, was born in one of Kenley's wooden huts. As far as I can remember, the new Mess was then in process of building but we were using the old Mess (Flintfield House) which lay just to the east of the present Mess. Fighting Area Headquarters moved to Uxbridge a few weeks after its formation.
>
> There are two things I always associate with Kenley, first that the pilots were more dashing than disciplined and second that the aerodrome surface gave continual trouble. But though I sometimes had to jump on junior pilots pretty heavily for breaking the flying regulations, I always enjoyed a visit to Kenley as A.O.C. or later A.O.C.-in-C. as there was a great esprit de corps about the place and a homely, friendly atmosphere; even after a pilot had received a good dressing down I felt that he went off smiling inwardly at the thought that his A.O.C. had once himself been a carefree pilot and understood the joys of power and speed under one's control.
>
> Kenley had several fatal accidents when I had Fighting Area, but these never damped the ardour of the pilots; most of the accidents were on Grebes, an aeroplane I never liked.

The gradual replacement of No 32 Squadron's obsolescent Snipes in 1925 by the Gloster Grebe naturally prompted the pilots to fly one against the other to make direct comparisons between the two. To their surprise, they discovered that the older machines could easily out-manoeuvre their latest mounts, but the superior speed of the Grebe more than compensated for this. The Grebe also had the facility of being able to carry four 20lb. bombs in racks under the wings, something which was later to cause an accident which gave rise to concern among people living nearby.

One evening, four Grebes took off armed with practice bombs, intent on practising for the following day's bombing competition. As they flew over Caterham, one of the pilots was astonished to see Pilot Officer Montgomery's machine release a bomb. He watched in horror as it fell

A char-a-banc outing for the airmen on 9th September, 1922. The journey cannot have a very comfortable one, judging from the vehicle's solid rubber tyres.

Surrey County Libraries

and hit a building in Caterham High Street. The unfortunate recipient of the missile was Allen's baker's shop; it passed right through the rear of the building, causing considerable damage and giving the residents, Mr and Mrs Colman, quite a shock. On returning, the machine in question was given a thorough inspection by ground staff but nothing was found to be wrong with it or with the bomb release.

The incident was given wide coverage in the national Press, and the local newspaper excelled with a very detailed account of the accident. An R.A.F. spokesman went to considerable lengths to reassure local people, explaining that this was the first time an accident of this nature had occurred and the possibility of it ever happening again was very remote. It is interesting to note, however, that at the bottom of the report the newspaper supplied the name and address of a reputable insurance company where adequate cover could be obtained against falling aeroplanes or pieces therefrom.* It would appear that the nation had more to fear from its own Air Force than from any other at this time.

Another young pilot who incurred official displeasure and put up what must be the most resounding "black" of 1926 was Pilot Officer

*This advertisement was used on other occasions when an incident involving aeroplanes was reported.

Holden, who looped a Grebe round the high-level walkway of Tower Bridge on Christmas Day. Group Captain N. W. F. Mason recalls:

On the day of the incident, no doubt as the result of some minor indiscretion of my own, I was carrying out the duties of Orderly Officer. On arrival at the Mess during the evening of the 25th, I was not in the least surprised to find Pilot Officer Holden and Pilot Officer Griffiths in dinner jackets, eagerly awaiting my return and expectantly waiting to hand over duties and proceed to town. I was, however, not a little surprised to hear that they had taken up the dual Grebe during the day, flown under the Tower Bridge, completing this manoeuvre by rolling off a loop, beaten up the crane at that time located on top of Swan and Edgars, and finally force landed on the way home to ask for the direction to Kenley. "The weather was a bit thick", remarked Holden. "But how did you get the aircraft restarted?" I asked. "Oh, we turned out the Guard", he replied.

I remember some days later a policeman who had been on point duty on Tower Bridge appearing as chief witness for the prosecution at the Court Martial. After a brief period in the Sergeants' Mess he was quite convinced in his own mind that the cloud ceiling on the day of the incident was down to the level of Tower Bridge. Holden was a remarkable fellow, and a delightful personality; quite fearless, possessor of a good brain, and an excellent all-round sportsman, giving a good account of himself on the rugger field. While he was under arrest, he would play to you on his violin, read to you in French, or any language in which you might be interested, or paint pictures for you, in fact, make your brief stay with him more enjoyable than that offered by the carefree Mess of the 1926 Kenley. My last remembrances of him were when he received a reprimand from the A.O.C. for flying in tight formation with a civilian airliner from Croydon and his voluntary delayed parachute jump at Biggin Hill where his delayed action was mercifully assisted by a drop of the level of the airfield.

I can remember frequently hearing stories of—but did not actually witness—the incidents when "Cod" Foster and Leslie Hamilton used to get the chaps to help them to prepare a Bristol Fighter to night fly to Eastchurch after a Dinner Night. Motor-cars used to provide flood lighting for the aerodrome, and they normally managed to make Eastchurch where they were landed under similar conditions of motor-car lights.

Soon after the incidents described by Group Captain Mason, Holden was leading a flight of Grebes practising formation flying and insisted that they were not close enough together, even though another machine had already touched his own. On the following flight, as the Grebes edged closer the same thing occurred again but this time they collided and Holden lost his life in the resulting crash.

The following June Charles Lindbergh flew in, fresh from his triumphant solo flight across the Atlantic. Although he only intended to stay for lunch, bad weather conditions prevented him continuing his journey to Paris and so he remained a guest until the following day when he departed with an escort of two Gamecocks, which left him at Lympne.

The death of Edmund Byron, local Lord of the Manor and owner of the Coulsdon Court estate, raised a large question mark over the future

An Armstrong Whitworth Siskin IIIA of No 32 Squadron at Kenley. The Siskin IIIA with its Armstrong Siddeley Jaguar IV engine was in service with the R.A.F. from 1926 to 1932.   *Mr Eugene Roux*

of Waterhouse Farm, the land on the other side of Hayes Lane, on the aerodrome's western boundary. This did not cause the R.A.F. any undue concern until a wire fence was erected across one of the adjoining fields in an area which had hitherto been regarded as an unofficial R.A.F. preserve, directly in line with their flight path.* When a large board appeared in the field advertising plots of land for private development, the casual interest shown by the Kenley fliers turned to dismay. Realising that legally they could do nothing to prevent building on the site, the Air Ministry decided that it would be best to buy the offending acreage. Then the idea that the whole of Waterhouse Farm should be purchased and the non-used area rented out as a small-holding gained approval. After the Treasury had agreed the money for the transaction and negotiations had been going on for some time, the agents announced that they had received an offer for the whole Coulsdon Court estate and were selling it to C. W. Neville, of the Coulsdon Heights Estate Company. On the completion of the transaction, the R.A.F. almost immediately started new negotiations for the purchase of 14½ acres, which was finalised during the latter part of 1927. Ironically, the Waterhouse Farm land had to be purchased by the R.A.F. for expansion and the diversion of Hayes Lane in 1939.

During 1927 No 24 Squadron moved away to Northolt and No 23 Squadron, under the command of Squadron Leader Raymond Colli-shaw, D.S.O., O.B.E., D.S.C., D.F.C., one of the really outstanding

*This flight path was vital to the D.H.9A bombers because, when taking off in that direction, they could not climb above the Handley Page sheds.

Gloster Gamecocks and airmen of No 23 Squadron in 1930. The Gamecock, the last biplane fighter of wooden construction to serve with the R.A.F., came into use with No 23 Squadron in 1926 and was not replaced by Bristol Bulldogs until 1931.

Surrey County Libraries

fighter pilots of the First World War, officially credited with sixty enemy aircraft destroyed, came to partner No 32 Squadron. No 23 was equipped with Gloster Gamecocks.

Air Commodore A. W. B. McDonald, C.B., A.F.C., was then a pilot with No 23 Squadron:

> I can remember Collishaw's private unsuccessful attempt to develop landing lights on aeroplanes, the intention being to dispense with the use of flares. He bought the most powerful motor-car headlights he could get and had them fixed on the undercarriage of a Gamecock: however, they didn't work very well and the attempt was eventually abandoned.
>
> Earlier, in 1926, Collishaw arranged to lead a squadron formation from Kenley to view the total eclipse of the sun from above the clouds near Liverpool. He only cancelled the take-off at the last moment because of heavy rain and 10/10th cloud at 500 feet. As we had no gyro instruments at all and only just enough petrol to get to Liverpool and land at Sealand immediately afterwards, I dread to think what would have happened had we taken off. However, such was our ignorance, mixed with enthusiasm, in those days, that we were all most disappointed not to go.

Air Vice-Marshal Willock, who commanded a squadron and later the Storage Park immediately after the war, returned as Station Commander in 1927:

> After my return from Egypt in 1926, I was posted to the Air Ministry as a squadron leader, and after I had been there only a few months Sir Philip Game came into my office and told me confidentially that I was going to be promoted on 1st January and that he wanted me to take command of Kenley Station. He explained that he thought it would be an uphill task as the fighter boys were obviously out of hand and spent far too much time in London at Mrs Meyrick's "43" Club, and the object of my posting was to make them toe the line and generally to ginger things up. Jones-Williams had by now taken over command of No 23 Squadron (Gamecocks) and Rex Mansell was in command of No 32 Squadron (Siskins).

Although tightening up of discipline became the rule, it would appear that even the Station Commander permitted himself the occasional departure from the dignity of his rank. C. G. Grey, arguably the most often quoted aviation journalist of the early days and editor of *The Aeroplane*, writes:

> My recollection of Kenley is dining there when R. P. Willock commanded the Station. What sticks in my memory most is that, late in the evening, the big arm-chairs were placed in a line from end to end of the ante-room and Willock took a header into the seat of the first, rolled (endwise) over the back into the second and so on for about ten or a dozen. Pretty good going for a wing commander; anyway, it certainly beat a lot of the youngsters.

Soon after taking up his appointment as Commanding Officer of No 23 Squadron, Jones-Williams contacted his friend Richard Atcherley and invited him to join the squadron. Atcherley's natural flying ability soon earned him the command of "C" Flight which he carefully moulded into a team worthy of acclaim at the Hendon Air Show. Although quite fearless, he did manage to give himself a moderate shaking on one occasion while attempting his first night landing in a Gamecock. During his final approach he suddenly lost sight of the aerodrome lights and was stunned by the realisation that he was too low and they were being obscured by the trees on the south-western boundary; he somehow managed to collide with the trees and still remain healthy enough to make a successful landing. His trick flying and hair-raising stunts, particularly when in America, plus an irrepressible personality, earned him the affectionate nickname "Batchy", a name which stuck with him throughout his career. He later became a member of the successful Schneider Trophy winning team and world speed record holder. During the Second World War he returned as Sector Commander.

Squadron Leader Jones-Williams was soon to perish with Flight Lieutenant Jenkins (mentioned earlier by Sir James Robb) while attempting the first non-stop flight to the Cape, their Fairey Napier long-range monoplane crashing in the Atlas Mountains on its outward journey from Cranwell. The vacant position at the head of the squadron left by the death of Jones-Williams was filled by H. W. Woollett, D.S.O., M.C., another of the First World War fighter aces.

By this time No 23 Squadron had established an enviable reputation for formation aerobatic flying, and in June, 1931, a team of three was selected for the Hendon Display consisting of Day and Bader, with Stephenson as substitute. The new routines introduced by Day, combined with fine exhibition flying, stole the show. Not long afterwards the squadron completed its conversion from Gamecocks to Bristol Bulldogs and, in attempting to impress a few spectators while on a visit to Woodley aerodrome, Douglas Bader misjudged a low level roll and crashed, resulting in the loss of both his legs. Hearing of his precarious state,

The Kenley sports day of 1928, from a picture postcard issued by a Caterham photographer.
Surrey County Libraries

fellow members of the squadron had a collection for a suitable floral tribute, the need for which became less as the days passed. The money was later spent on a celebration party to mark Bader's return to good health. His fight to overcome his adversity and to return to the R.A.F. and flying during the Second World War is now a well known story.

In 1931 J. B. Edwards, the Whyteleafe building and civil engineering contractor,* commenced a rebuilding programme which would establish Kenley purely as a fighter station, maintaining two squadrons on a permanent basis. In September, the resident squadrons departed to Biggin Hill while the necessary demolition and rebuilding, which

---

*This company had strong associations with the aerodrome, having earlier built married quarters and the Operations block (after first building a prototype at Uxbridge). Over a period of several years, they also re-roofed the 1917 sheds, replacing the original asbestos sheets with tongued and grooved boarding covered with bituminous felt.

included barrack blocks, sergeants' mess, stores and a Naafi, was undertaken.

Air Commodore G. B. Dacre, C.B.E., D.S.O., (a pre-1914 pilot) was then in command and recalled that as he was leaving the deserted station to the mercy of "Works and Buildings" he happened to pass a steam roller and a gang of men who were busily repairing a road which had been in a bad condition for a long time. It occurred to him that the road did not figure as a road in the new plan. Somewhat puzzled, he returned to ask why they were bothering to repair it; the workmen said that the work had just been authorised and had to be completed before the road was taken up. An even more bewildered Air Commodore continued on his way, possibly regretting having stopped to inquire.

The curtain went down on flying for twenty months, during which time the aerodrome reverted to being a Storage Section (somewhat reminiscent of the role it had played in earlier days), as work progressed on the new buildings.

Station Headquarters was re-formed in May, 1934, under Wing Commander G. S. M. Insall, V.C., M.C., and Nos 3 and 17 Squadrons, equipped with Bristol Bulldogs, moved in from Upavon. Both units flying the same type of aeroplane increased the competitive spirit between them, and each cast an ever-watchful, critical eye over the

Members of No 23 Squadron aerobatic team posing in front of a Gloster Gamecock. They are, left to right, Douglas Bader, M. M. Day and Stephenson (reserve). The display they gave at the R.A.F. Pageant at Hendon in June, 1931, well demonstrated the aerobatic prowess of the Gamecock. *Surrey County Libraries*

activities of the other. Group Captain E. P. Mackay, then a Flight Commander in No 3 Squadron, gives some indication of the feeling between them as he tells of their wickedly gleeful response to one of the misfortunes which befell their opposite number:

> I can well remember Squadron Leader F. J. Vincent, who was commanding No 17 (F) Squadron, bringing in his squadron of Bulldogs in a formation landing on the not very big aerodrome of those days. It was a lovely landing but unfortunately the Sergeant Pilot on Vincent's right slightly overshot and started swerving into his C.O. The latter applied his brakes rather too vigorously and turned ack over tock, much to the joy of us in No 3 Squadron.

The rivalry finally ended when Squadron Leader Martyn took No 3 Squadron overseas to Port Sudan in October, 1935, at the time of the Abyssinian Crisis. Meanwhile, with growing apprehension about German military strength, the R.A.F. set about a comprehensive examination and subsequent reorganisation of the country's air defence structure which finally resulted in the formation of Fighter Command. As part of the general build-up, the forming of new squadrons gained a high priority.

June, 1936, saw the birth of a squadron which was of special importance in the aerodrome's history. Under Squadron Leader A. Vere-Harvey, No 615 Squadron, Auxiliary Air Force, came into existence and was given the title "County of Surrey". Almost from the very first, Winston Churchill showed a keen interest in its fortunes and agreed to become its honorary Air Commodore. Later, during the Second World War, the men and machines of the squadron fought almost to a standstill in defence of the aerodrome which they always regarded as home.

Other squadrons were formed by budding off flights from existing units and using them as a nucleus of experienced personnel on which to build. On 3rd September, 1936, "B" Flight of No 17 Squadron was detached and from it No 46 Squadron was re-formed, and a few months later, on 15th March, 1937, "B" Flight of No 17 was once more split away to become the basis of No 80 Squadron, which immediately moved to Hendon with Gloster Gauntlets.

While this reorganisation was in progress, the aerodrome was also undergoing a major alteration. The large hangar built along Hayes Lane at the outset to house long-range Vickers and Handley Page bombers had been little used for some time and remained a nuisance and hazard to pilots, so it was decided to demolish it, leaving the western boundary free from buildings and obstructions.

The sequence of events during the period preceding the outbreak of the Second World War has a strong sense of the absurd about it. Only fifteen weeks before the Munich Crisis in September, 1938, when the nation's defences were put on a war footing, pending the outcome of

Members of No 3 Squadron pose for the photographer in 1936. They had been the first squadron to receive the Bristol Bulldog in June, 1929, and were soon, in March, 1937, to re-equip with the Gloster Gladiator. *Surrey County Libraries*

talks between Prime Minister Chamberlain and Hitler, Messrs Reickhoff, Veltheim and Pettalbach, members of a German Air Mission, were entertained and given V.I.P. treatment while visiting the station. The only area shielded from the prying eyes of the "guests" appears to have been the Operations Room. They no doubt reported favourably on the lack of modern aircraft; only biplanes were in evidence on the day.

At the time of the Munich Crisis telephone lines were connected up to feed Kenley information from Observer Corps centres if the need arose. The state of preparedness of the resident squadrons gave some food for thought. No 3 Squadron was having trouble with camouflaging its Gladiators through not having the paint to do it; this was solved by sending someone down to a shop in Whyteleafe for some household distemper. The engines of No 17 Squadron's Gauntlets were warmed up and apparently ready for an emergency until someone asked about ammunition for their guns; on inquiry it was discovered that it was not

An aerial photograph of Kenley taken about 1931–32. Hayes Lane and the Handley Page sheds can be seen at lower left.   *Surrey County Libraries*

immediately available, so they stood down until some was located and belted up. The other home squadron, No 615 Squadron, moved to Old Sarum to make way for the incoming Demons of No 600 Squadron from Hendon.

With the successful conclusion of the talks between Prime Minister Neville Chamberlain and German Chancellor Adolf Hitler, the squadrons reverted to their normal state, and it was with thanksgiving and no small measure of relief that toasts were drunk to what later turned out to be only a temporary peace.

Equipping No 3 Squadron with Hawker Hurricanes earlier in the year* had clearly shown the size limitations of the aerodrome when used by the new generation of eight-gun monoplane fighters. Spectators stood with bated breath during the final seconds of their comparatively long

*They were the second squadron to receive the new type (March, 1938).

42

take-off run until the aircraft finally staggered into the air, just clearing the bushes on the outer perimeter.* At this time Hurricanes were equipped with the old-fashioned two-bladed, fixed-pitch wooden propellers, which were inefficient and necessitated a long take-off run. This certainly had some bearing on the decision to pass on the machines to No 73 Squadron at Digby for them to familiarise themselves with the new type, leaving the Kenley pilots to renew their association with the Gladiator biplane.

The threat of war continued to hang over Europe and early the following year it was considered desirable to bring the Royal Air Force Volunteer Reserve into active service, and some thirty men were called to spend two or three evenings each week training and practising Operations Room duties. When the time came, they were to supplement the group of twelve or so regular airmen and make possible an "around the clock" shift system of trained men.

Flying Officer Pat Lister was appointed acting flight lieutenant with responsibilities for the final shakedown of the Operations Room organisation. He recalls that one of the part-time airmen under training that summer was Sergeant Bill Huggett, who in civilian life had the good fortune to be a director of Ex-Lax, the pharmaceutical company, and his mode of transport befitted one of such standing. During the warm evenings, Pat and his fellow officers sat with the Mess windows open, gazing with envious eyes upon the apparent quality of Huggett's splendid, if somewhat elderly, Rolls Royce; the inevitable comparison with their own less ostentatious vehicles parked nearby became the source of much comment and led to the obviously well-breeched sergeant being regarded with some awe.

Girls were recruited into the W.A.A.F. Mrs S. Hancock, née Thatcher, joined at this time:

After overcoming my mother's misgivings, I signed on at the recruiting centre during one of the Empire Air Days. Every Thursday afternoon the other girls and I arrived at the aerodrome for training, the organisation of which was a bit sketchy because at that stage no one knew exactly what role we were training for. They asked if we had any particular skills and when I told them I could drive I became a driver, although there was nothing to drive.

One thing we were introduced to was drilling, and to the accompaniment of big smiles and humorous remarks from the men, who became a regular audience and seemed to think the girls were being paraded for their entertainment, we marched up and down in front of the hangars.

With no uniform, dress was optional and I suppose we represented a fairly broad spectrum of the fashion of the day, including on one occasion a girl turning up

---

*One aircraft stalled on take-off and was badly damaged; five days later, another stalled at 200 feet on its landing approach, killing the pilot, Pilot Officer Henry May.

during the cold weather in a beautiful silver fox fur. For me it was something more suitable like a straight black skirt, but there were problems.

I remember one afternoon we were drilling, all in step, arms swinging in perfect harmony, when I felt one of the straps break on my slip. The other one snapped as the parade was coming to a halt, but not me; knowing that a minor disaster was imminent and the slip would drop around my ankles, I had to make a decision. "Halt!" came the command, and as everyone stopped, I kept on marching; regular step, arms swinging, head up, eyes straight ahead. They stood agog as I continued in a straight line and disappeared off the parade ground. What they didn't see was the hasty dash round behind a hangar where I effected repairs.

Training of the Volunteer Reserve into an efficient staff at this time enabled their full mobilisation to run reasonably smoothly, and allowed an influx of untrained personnel to be hastily absorbed and trained by them later on. When war came, the shortage of staff was so great that W.A.A.F.s were drafted in after only ten days' basic training; in some cases, even at that late stage, before they had received their uniforms.

Commencing in May, 1934, the Empire Air Days became an increasingly popular annual event, providing entertainment for aviation enthusiasts and local populace alike. They culminated in the display on 20th May, 1939, when the airmen showed off the various aircraft of the day before a very large crowd. It heralded the end of the biplane era; although not much in evidence on the day, the Hurricane and Spitfire had already arrived and had begun to supersede them. The demand for programmes was such that they had all been sold in the first two hours, and people who left early found a ready market for their second-hand specimens.

Most doors were open, enabling the public to view the different

Left: A Gloster Gauntlet, its engine running, demonstrates its twin Vickers machine-guns at the butts during an Empire Air Day about 1938. *Mr J. W. L. Goldsmith*

Opposite: All heads turn to watch a Gloster Gauntlet of No 46 (F) Squadron taking off at the 1937 Empire Air Day. In the foreground is Hayes Lane. *Surrey County Libraries*

trades and skills employed in the working of the Station. In the aircraft maintenance area, an aircraft had been partially stripped of its outer covering, permitting a clear view of the functioning of its controls. Machine shops, engine testing facilities, the forge and tinsmiths' departments were all open to view. In one hangar, personnel demonstrated their skill in parachute folding and another hangar housed a Link Trainer, in which pilots learned instrument-flying techniques and gained experience while still on the ground. Barrack rooms, station sick quarters, dining hall and cookhouse, each withstood its share of the thousands of interested people who passed through during the course of the day.

At the firing butts, next to No 2 Hangar, a 615 Squadron Gauntlet provided the noisiest feature of the afternoon when it stood with its engine racing to operate the firing mechanism of its twin Vickers machine-guns. The exciting, ear-piercing noise created by the short bursts of gunfire was impressive to the casual observer, but in Air Ministry circles it had already been realised that it would require a minimum of eight machine-guns to achieve conclusive results in the high-speed engagements of future air warfare.

The afternoon's flying display included a number of items which had become popular over the years, e.g. an aircraft diving down and hooking up written messages suspended on a line between two poles stuck in the ground; dropping supplies from the air, etc. Members of the public were given the opportunity of using radio-telephony to give directions to the pilot of an aircraft which was flying overhead. When told what to do, he immediately put the aircraft into the suggested

The Gloster Gauntlets of No 17 (F) Squadron are much in evidence in this
view of Kenley on Empire Air Day, 1937.   *Surrey County Libraries*

manoeuvre. All instructions were followed to the letter, until a lady asked
for a low flight over the aerodrome with the pilot singing "The Chestnut
Tree". He sped low over the field but declined the opportunity to
demonstrate his vocal ability. Perhaps he considered the sixpence paid by
the lady was insufficient to warrant him setting the whole thing to music.

The antics of a "pupil" pilot, following his instructor's flying pattern
in a similar machine, caused many smiles when he got into a terrible
mix-up and finished up by doing loops and rolls the wrong way round.
After a while it dawned on most people that the pupil's clever cavorting
about in the air could have been performed only by a very experienced
man.

The grand flypast included Tutor, Magister, Hart, Hector, Gauntlet,
Gladiator, Harvard, Wellington, Lysander, Battle (a fine formation of
twenty-four had flown past earlier in the day) and, bringing up the rear,
the splendid sight of a lone Hurricane racing over the aerodrome.

At the end of the afternoon the crowd, having slaked its aviation
thirst, slowly drifted away. They had experienced the thrills, noise and
smells associated with aeroplanes, and those more fortunate had been on

five-shilling pleasure flights over the surrounding countryside in a de Havilland Rapide owned by Air Despatch. The majority had been content just to watch the flying, most of which was performed by the Gladiator and Gauntlet biplanes.

Shortly after the air display No 17 Squadron moved to North Weald, leaving No 615 Squadron as the only resident squadron, No 3 Squadron having already gone to Biggin Hill at the beginning of the month.

Preparations were in hand for extensive alterations and extensions to the aerodrome which would enable Hurricanes and Spitfires to operate more easily and effectively. The worry of pedestrians and vehicles travelling along Hayes Lane was removed at last;* by Act of Parliament the lane, which had remained a public thoroughfare across the flying field for twenty-two years, was diverted to a wide loop to the west, the Air Ministry having to purchase Waterhouse Farm for this purpose. During August, contractors commenced work on laying concrete runways and a perimeter track. Hangars 1, 2 and 4 were regarded as unnecessary and were to be demolished, leaving only four of the original seven of 1917 vintage.

*Earlier, while using the road over the aerodrome, an old man had been knocked off the top of a haycart and killed in an unfortunate incident with an aeroplane.

CHAPTER THREE

Into Battle

A T THE outbreak of war on 3rd September, No 615 Squadron prepared to move to Croydon, leaving Kenley hors de combat without aircraft. They were almost immediately joined there by their colleagues of No 17 Squadron and No 3 Squadron, both having equipped with Hurricanes while away from the Sector.

The fact that Kenley was non-operational at such an important time and waiting for concrete runways to be laid is perhaps surprising, when for all its life the aerodrome surface had been known to be poor because of bad drainage. It had also been known for some time that operating modern aircraft in the restricted aerodrome space did not leave much margin for error. Perhaps the answer to the question can be found in Robert Wright's book *Dowding and the Battle of Britain*. He writes: "During the winter of 1936–37, Dowding recalled, there were three consecutive weeks during which not a single aircraft could take off or land at Kenley. This was one of his (Dowding's) most important airfields; but Dowding explained. The Air Staff fought against this vital need for all-weather runways because an imported Army Staff Officer had devised a system of camouflaging aerodromes and he said that the addition of such runways would spoil it."

At the outbreak of hostilities, the Royal Air Force Volunteer Reserve was immediately mobilised and soon soldiers of the 12th Battalion, Royal Fusiliers arrived for aerodrome defence duties with others from the Honourable Artillery Company.

While construction work was in progress, the Hurricanes of No 3 Squadron at Croydon used Manston on the Kent coast as an advanced base for defensive patrols over ships engaged in laying protective minefields offshore. They were successfully controlled from an emergency Operations Room set up at Hawkinge, the system working well until control was switched from there to Kenley. The first attempt proved disastrous and a very quick and positive condemnation came from the pilots concerned. Later, an inquiry found that at the time G.P.O. engineers had been testing and correcting faults on the telephone lines, and it was their interference which had caused the breakdown in communications. A lesson had been learned that was not forgotten. In the years ahead, those responsible for communications held the fate of the country's air defence in their hands.

On 15th November, in company with No 607 Squadron, No 615 Squadron left Croydon for Merville, France. Groundstaff were transported in airliners of Imperial Airways which had been taken over at the outbreak of war. Most of the forty passengers in the old biplane *Syrinx* were sick during the bumpy two-hour flight. On arrival they were shown to an old grain silo where they filled mattresses with straw and bedded down on the floor; conditions not too far removed from what they had experienced at Croydon, where they had been sleeping on the floor of a hangar. Officers were billeted with French people in the nearby town.

No 615 Squadron's Gladiators were to function as part of the Air Component of the British Expeditionary Force. An accident a few days earlier had robbed them of Pilot Officer Rose, killed when he flew into the side of the chalk pit at Chaldon.

At home, any optimistic thoughts the civilian locals had about continuing to use the newly completed Hayes Lane diversion road were quickly dispelled when barriers were put up at each end, blocking off the entire section. The only exceptions to these strictures were Mr and Mrs Robbins, who lived in Waterhouse Lane, a track off the new road, which was their only access to Kenley, and Mr Bestow, who was allowed to

Gloster Gladiators of No 615 (County of Surrey) Squadron, Royal Auxiliary Air Force, at summer camp at Ford in 1939.   *Mr Eugene Roux*

continue his bee-keeping enterprise in a field close by and regularly came to tend the hives. They were each provided with a special pass for use at the northern barrier near Old Lodge Lane. Like most other people living within a radius of one thousand yards of the aerodrome, they had been advised by the authorities to move away at the outbreak of war, but had chosen to stay. Their self-imposed discipline of never talking about anything they saw or heard while going about their daily business would

Left: Members of No 615 (County of Surrey) Squadron, Royal Auxiliary Air Force, at summer camp at Ford in August, 1939. Soon after this photograph was taken they were hastily recalled to Kenley as it became clear that war was approaching.
Mr Eugene Roux

Opposite: Ground staff ponder the problems posed by a Gloster Gladiator's unhappy landing.
Mr J. W. L. Goldsmith

have done credit to the military itself. Mr and Mrs Robbins did move in 1941, but were allowed to return before the end of the war.

The picture of the role Kenley was to play in the defence of the country was now complete. When Fighter Command was first conceived during reorganisation of the R.A.F. in 1936 the country had been divided into two, responsibility for each of these areas falling to a fighter group, the South of England to No 11 Group and the Midlands and North to No 12. Further divisions occurred later, resulting in the formation of No 13 Group, which took over the North, and No 10 which looked after the South-west. Several premier fighter stations in each Group were to control the operation of other aerodromes in a clearly defined area or "Sector", and so it was that by 1939 Kenley was headquarters of "B" Sector in No 11 Group covering an area with a boundary that crossed the South Coast at Middleton and followed a straight line to Virginia Water, turning eastwards to Hampton, Petersham and West Wickham and finally returning over the coast in a straight

line through Bexhill. In the Sector the aerodromes at Croydon, Redhill and Gatwick and, later, those at Shoreham and Friston all became satellites* under Kenley control. West Malling, in Kent, was also a satellite.†

An Operations Room communications system for ground-to-air control of fighter aircraft had direct telephone links with the Filter Room at Fighter Command Headquarters, Stanmore, and the Observer Corps

*See Appendix two.

†Surprisingly, there is no record of this in the Kenley Operations Record Book. It was to serve as a forward aerodrome for Kenley and Biggin Hill and was utilised mostly for night fighters.

The Sector Operations building on the aerodrome at Kenley, from which the Fighter Control system was moved away on 3rd September, 1940. This historic building was demolished in 1980. *Author*

centres at Winchester, Horsham, Watford, Bromley and Maidstone. Direction finding stations at Farthing Down, Lewes and Marden supplied readings from which the position of the airborne aircraft could be determined so that ground control could give them guidance. Group headquarters at Uxbridge decided initial deployment of aircraft.

The control system worked in this manner. An interwoven chain of radar stations sited on the coast (known as C.H. or Chain Home) scanned out to sea and into French air space, each picking up information on aerial activity within its field of vision over a range of one hundred miles. Their findings were passed back to the Filter Room at Stanmore, where knowledge of British aircraft movements enabled the staff to decide whether the aircraft in question was friendly or hostile. If the latter, immediately the aircraft flew inland over the coast and moved behind the radar surveillance its progress was monitored by members of the Observer Corps, a volunteer body of men and women mostly working out in the open at small lookout posts, using little more than their eyes and ears to record the vital information. When contact was made, they telephoned the details of type and, if more than one, number of aircraft, estimated height and direction, etc., to their own Observer Corps centres which in turn relayed the information simultaneously to the Group Operations Room at Uxbridge and to Sector Stations, where the course of the aircraft was plotted on a large table map. As can be seen, theoretically the radar supplied the early warning, giving defending fighters sufficient time to take off and be in an advantageous position when an interception became possible; and the Observer Corps was responsible for tracking and recording progress of enemy aircraft when activity was centred overland, enabling some speculation as to possible target and intervention.

To establish the relative positions of the defending fighters, a system known as "pip squeak" (so called because of the peculiar sound emitted by a small device incorporated in the aircraft's radio telephone transmitter) was evolved. A sixty-second clock on the wall of the Operations Room was divided into four equal divisions, each of fifteen seconds. Soon after he had taken off, the pilot switched on his transmitter on a given verbal signal from the Operations Room so that his allotted fifteen-second transmitting time directly coincided with a designated section of the clock. For fourteen of his fifteen seconds his set would automatically transmit, remaining silent for the rest of the minute while the other aircraft on the clock each in turn did likewise. These transmissions were picked up by the three direction finding stations and their readings forwarded to the Sector Operations Room for the duty crew to calculate the aircraft's position. As the information from each station was phoned in, it was called out to people on the direction finding table who placed arms (later strings) across a table map of the area. By using the location of each station as a point of reference related to the reported bearing of the aircraft's transmission signal, where the three arms crossed on the map was the estimated position of the aircraft. The technique had to be used quickly, because the speed of aircraft could be anything up to five or six miles a minute and every second counted.

This system enabled the controller to know the whereabouts of his aircraft, be it flying alone or as one of a section or squadron; it only required the one transmitting aircraft to establish the position of the bunch. A similar system had been employed for many years at Croydon Airport to assist civilian aircraft with their navigation.

Knowing the relative position of friend and foe, the controller could then effect an interception. Once in the air, the Spitfires and Hurricanes were under his guidance, and it required a person with special qualities to do the job well. How the controller conducted his affairs could make the difference between life and death to the men in the air.

The whole ground control network was woven together by direct telephone lines, and it was the G.P.O. who bonded the entire organisation together. Their civilian engineers were to make a significant contribution to the defence of the country. Very soon, and certainly during the Battle of Britain period, British Intelligence began to play an increasingly important part in the air defence system by supplying Fighter Command with information gained from speedily decoded German radio transmissions.

Kenley was responsible for the air defence of a large region of South-east England, with a southernmost limit extending to the English Channel, on the other side of which France itself was committed to an uncertain future. To the north of the Sector was London, the capital city and centre of the country's business and commercial interests; in the mind of any adversary, because of its size and importance, probably regarded as a prime and vulnerable target. Three, sometimes four, front line fighter squadrons were to form the basis of the Sector's defence, two based at Kenley and the others at the nearby civil airport at Croydon.

Work progressed on the two all-weather concrete runways (extended in 1943), one running from south-east to north-west, the other crossing it south-west to north-east. To provide access to them, the perimeter track (not to be completed until early April, 1940, due to bad weather) wound its way around the outer areas of the flying field. The ability of the all-metal fighter to stand up to the rigours of the weather (as opposed to its atmospherically sensitive wooden predecessor) had been exploited and twelve blast pens, each capable of holding three aircraft,* were positioned at various intervals off the perimeter track, so that aircraft could be dispersed as widely as possible around the aerodrome. Two of them were built off the outer side of the defunct Hayes Lane, which had been brought well within the aerodrome boundary. The back of each blast pen contained an air raid shelter as an integral part of its structure for the protection of ground staff when under attack.

Barbed wire and slit trenches were becoming commonplace; pill boxes and gunposts were constructed at strategic points. Later, at the time of the Battle of Britain, the strength of the defences was not great. The only modern anti-aircraft guns were four 40mm Bofors of 31st Battery, 11th Light Anti-Aircraft Regiment (which were taken over by

---

*Later, in practice, it was usually two aircraft; the remainder were usually dispersed on the grass in convenient positions near the perimeter track.

their colleagues of 51st Regiment during the latter part of August). These were supported by a collection of somewhat ancient weapons. Light calibre Lewis guns, veterans of an earlier age of warfare, served a dual purpose as anti-aircraft weapons and for defence against attack by enemy parachute and ground forces. These were manned by R.A.F. gunners and men of 148th Battery, 43rd Light Anti-Aircraft Regiment, who also had in their charge two elderly three-inch guns which were not ideally suitable for aerodrome defence, both requiring some inventiveness on the part of the gunners to make them effective; an open sight was made out of reinforcing wire and carefully fitted to the guns so that they could be brought into action. The effectiveness of these two weapons was looked upon with much scepticism. What did not help was the restriction imposed on any shooting practice, due to a shortage of ammunition; it was not lifted until 12th September. Another adaptation was a 20mm Hispano aircraft cannon.

A recently developed device known as Parachute and Cable had been installed. This was basically an electrically activated rocket fired into the air, dragging a long length of cable after it. It was hoped that as the cable slowly descended to earth beneath a parachute it would form a barrier in the path of a low-flying aircraft, which when it flew into it would activate another parachute at the lower end of the cable; the combined weight of cable and drag of both parachutes would bring the aircraft down. Three batteries, each consisting of twenty-five rockets set in three rows of eight or nine at 60 feet intervals, were installed at convenient sites away from the flying field on the north, north-west and south-west boundaries of the aerodrome. These were operated by R.A.F. personnel, usually Aircraftmen 2nd Class.

To prevent the aerodrome falling into enemy hands, members of D Company, 12 (HD) Battalion, Queen's Royal Regiment had moved in during May, taking up defensive positions and also doing general security duties with the H.A.C. It had been planned that if reinforcements were required a detachment of the Holding Company, Scots Guards, stationed three-quarters of a mile away at Caterham Barracks, should be moved in at a moment's notice (this call came very soon; they arrived with their own equipment, which included Bren and Lewis guns, on 10th May). Supplementing the Army's firepower, the R.A.F. supplied Lee Enfield rifles and one or two Lewis guns to a number of airmen in the hope that they would cope if attacked. Aerodrome defence was later taken over by the R.A.F. Regiment, when that unit was formed later in the war. This was the strength they were to achieve by the time Battle of Britain was fought; as the building contractors moved out, the defenders quickly moved into position.

On the Continent the war was going badly for the Allies. German attacks were of such ferocity that the invading forces advanced rapidly. Their advance gained such momentum that it halted only after they had pushed right through France and reached the English Channel.

The fortunes of No 615 Squadron had been as bad as those of the rest of the Allied forces; although they had been able to improve their potency by disposing of the ancient Gladiators and re-equipping with Hurricanes, they too were rapidly overwhelmed. The sudden decision to evacuate from Belgium and return home on 20th May was out of necessity rather than choice. The situation was so bad that the aerodrome at Moorseele had become untenable, and in the early hours of what turned out to be their final day in Belgium they moved to Norron Fontes. The measure of German air superiority was shown when a call came for an attack on an armed column entering Arras; out of Nos 615, 504 and

The pill box gunpost which can be seen under attack in the German picture on page 71. In the background can be seen the blast pen where the No 64 Squadron Spitfire was standing in the same photograph. All these were demolished in 1984.   *Author*

607 Squadrons, only twelve fit pilots could be called upon, and three of these failed to return from the sortie. Having checked their earlier base to ensure all the unflyable aircraft were destroyed, not burned for fear that the smoke would attract enemy aircraft down to investigate, Squadron Leader Kayll led his battle-weary squadron home to Kenley in the evening. The ground crews arrived back the next day via Boulogne on the cross-channel steamer *Canterbury* and camped at Tidworth overnight before proceeding to Croydon; No 607 Squadron arrived the same day.

It so happened that No 3 Squadron had also been withdrawn to Kenley, which provided Station Commander Tom Prickman with an outsize problem of finding accommodation for this unexpected influx of men, the Station's own quarters already being filled by the two resident squadrons. Some of Joe Kayll's men eventually found themselves housed in a girls' school at Croydon which, although somewhat spartan, must have felt the height of luxury after the trials of the previous few weeks. Some pilots found places in the Surrey Hills Hotel at Caterham, which was also a favoured residence of wives and girlfriends.

Having been starved of first-hand news from the Continent, people at Kenley were sceptical about the stories being told by the returned pilots of how serious the situation was over there and of the number of aircraft the Luftwaffe had been able to put into the air. When told of the tactics the squadron had been compelled to employ just to survive, they took the view that 615 Squadron was only an Auxiliary squadron that really did not know what they were talking about and had not put up a very good show anyway. This fatuous judgment was refuted a few days later when the truth was crushingly brought home to them on the beaches of Dunkirk; they then listened more intently and revised air fighting tactics to make use of the hard-won experience gained by the squadron. Within three days of their homecoming, while Hurricane strength was being restored, some of the pilots reverted to flying outmoded Gladiators in a hastily formed "G" Flight which operated from Manston for a week under the leadership of Flight Lieutenant Sanders, D.F.C.

Flying at Kenley had recommenced at the end of January, 1940, before the runways, taxiing tracks and other rebuilding work was completed; reconstruction had been seriously delayed by bad weather. The Hurricanes of No 3 Squadron were out on patrol over the English Channel protecting troopships whenever flying conditions permitted; in May they too would be on the Continent. At the end of March a flight of Blenheims from No 604 Squadron arrived and in early May No 253 Squadron was in residence for a few days with Hurricanes. It was not until 16th May, when Squadron Leader Aeneas (Don) MacDonell flew in with No 64 Squadron, that the flying field was considered suitable to receive Spitfires.

Based on the theory that it was better to lose half a squadron and to use the remainder as a nucleus on which to rebuild than to lose everyone, once or twice a composite unit made up from elements of Nos 253 and 111 Squadrons worked from Kenley, re-arming and re-fuelling during the day at bases in France before returning in the evening; they also sustained heavy losses in action against the now-dominant Luftwaffe. On 18th May only five aircraft out of twelve returned, most of the remainder having been caught and destroyed on the ground at Vitry-en-Artois (near Douai) as they prepared to leave for home. The French were pressing for more British fighter squadrons to be sent to France but, if this is an indication of the conditions there, it is perhaps doubtful they would have been able to survive long on the ground.

At the time of the desperate evacuation of the British Expeditionary Force from the beaches of Dunkirk, full operational flying was in progress, the resident squadrons making an important contribution to the air cover holding off the Luftwaffe. It was a period of intense activity, with squadrons being directed to and from the most convenient bases. During the last two days of May, no fewer than seven squadrons had aircraft operating from the Sector; some returning to Kenley, others moving to alternative aerodromes which were better placed. For the first time, the Luftwaffe and the R.A.F. met on equal terms and the ferocity of the fighting was a clear indication of the future.

In June most organised resistance in France and the Low Countries ceased. With Norway also in German hands, the Luftwaffe was able to raid any part of the British Isles, forcing a major redeployment of Fighter Command resources and the setting up of two new groups. The Kenley/Tangmere Sector boundary in 11 Group was moved in an easterly direction to a point near Shoreham during the July reorganisation.

King George VI came to Kenley and decorated Squadron Leader Kayll with the D.S.O. and D.F.C. Flight Lieutenant Sanders, a fellow pilot with No 615 Squadron, was also decorated with the Distinguished Flying Cross.

CHAPTER FOUR

The Battle of Britain

THE surrender of France and the Low Countries brought the Luftwaffe much nearer to the shores of Britain. Where it had been reasonable to assume that raids on England would only be carried out by bombers capable of considerable range, in the main unescorted, the new situation in Europe meant that even London was within easy reach of the bombers and was just within the range of the superb Messerschmitt Bf.109 single-seater fighter. This factor was of considerable significance; unescorted bombers were relatively easy meat for the Hurricanes and Spitfires, but the presence of the Messerschmitt Bf.109s changed all that. Whether used as escort or in a more tactical role, their influence would be considerable, even though constrained by limited fuel capacity.

The opening days of July, 1940, saw minor skirmishes with the Luftwaffe as they began to develop a strategy which they hoped would result in a seaborne invasion of Southern England. The success of the operation depended on their gaining air supremacy over the invasion area and, to some extent, on their ability to cope with the warships of the Royal Navy. Fighter Command was to be destroyed in the air by bringing the Spitfires and Hurricanes up into battle when and where the German airmen chose.

While small numbers of German aircraft made tentative raids on Southern England, it was over the English Channel that the first major clashes occurred between the Luftwaffe and British fighters providing air cover for shipping passing through the narrow seaway. A Dornier reconnaissance aircraft had a look at Kenley aerodrome on 3rd July and scattered a few bombs which caused superficial damage nearby. It quickly departed before anyone could hamper its progress, and got as far as Maidstone where No 32 Squadron found it on its way home. Convoy protection and raids on coastal targets provided a major part of the squadron's work for the rest of the month and, when No 64 Squadron's Spitfires were not involved, they kept their hand in by flying offensive patrols looking for trouble.

On 12th July, Prime Minister Winston Churchill, together with 11 Group Commander Keith Park, visited the Station while on a tour of Fighter Command aerodromes. The Prime Minister left for Northolt in his personal Flamingo aircraft, accompanied by Keith Park in a Hurricane.

Ten days after their return from Belgium, No 615 Squadron had once more become fully operational, being mostly engaged in shipping protection and flying offensive patrols, using either Hawkinge or Tangmere for convenience. Defending a convoy running the gauntlet through the English Channel on 14th July provided them with a major action, when nearly forty Junkers 87 Stuka dive-bombers, under the protection of a Messerschmitt Bf.109 escort, attacked the ships.* This engagement was recorded for posterity by B.B.C. commentator Charles

A Hawker Hurricane I of the first batch to enter service, with two-bladed wooden airscrew and fabric-covered mainplanes.
Gordon Kinsey

Gardiner as he stood in a grandstand position on the Cliffs of Dover and made his now-famous blow-by-blow commentary on the action out at sea.

Patrols over convoys highlighted the shortcomings of the "Pip squeak" High Frequency radio system used in locating the whereabouts of the British fighters. When they were low down over the water, direction finding stations began experiencing extreme difficulty in picking up their transmissions. Lack of height also put them below the operational scope of the coastal radar and no assistance could be gained from this. Deciding the whereabouts of the aircraft under such circumstances made life difficult in the Operations Room and led to much inspired guesswork by the duty crew.

To make possible an earlier response to German activity, a Kenley Sector squadron was regularly sent down to Hawkinge aerodrome, perched on high ground at the back of Folkestone on the Kent coast. Although not in the home Sector, its forward position was considered to be of sufficient tactical importance to warrant the move. At the time German activity was usually confined to low and medium height attacks against shipping, making a lengthy climb to intercept them unnecessary. The squadron got airborne at first light and stayed down at the coast until relieved either at midday or in the evening. In the event of trouble,

*Both Pilot Officer Montgomery and Flying Officer P. Collard were killed in this action.

they were the first to be sent up and they were also favourably placed to provide escorts for bombers striking at invasion barges in Calais.

When word was sent from Hawkinge that the squadron had taken off for home, Kenley Operations Room would call them up on the R/T and ask, "Are you coming by train?" The reply usually came back "Affirmative". This strange exchange of words indicated that pilots were following the railway track which runs in an almost straight line from Ashford to Redhill. A northwards change of course at Godstone, and the Caterham by-pass guided them on to the Kenley circuit.

The by-pass's distinctive white concrete surface, with Wapses Lodge roundabout at the northern end, pointed the way to the aerodrome's back door, but obviously it also had disadvantages; enemy pilots were equally capable of benefiting from its well-defined path. Knowing of this concern, the authorities did their best to camouflage the road by tar-spraying and using two different colours of grit to produce a patchy effect. The roundabout was also camouflaged but, standing out like the hub of a wheel, it could still be clearly seen from the air.

"Coming by train" did have its dangers, in peace as in war. In 1937 Pilot Officer Vickery was following the Ashford to Redhill railway line in a Gladiator of No 3 Squadron and, because of bad weather, was flying very low, just a few feet above the track. Suddenly, immediately ahead, the entrance to the tunnel north of Oxted appeared out of the murk with high ground above it (he had forgotten this). Yanking back on the stick, he put the aircraft into a steep climb, but with insufficient speed it stalled and fell on to the sharply rising hill above the tunnel. The only hurt to Vickery was a sprained ankle and a dent in his pride, but it took a very long time to retrieve the damaged aircraft from its precarious position.

A careful watch on the German-held Channel ports showed a steady advancement of invasion preparations, making everyone very much aware of the gravity of the situation. People had now become more alert to the danger of parachutists and watchful for infiltrators; and were encouraged to regard anything or anyone unusual with suspicion. Infringements of the nightly "blackout" regulations were treated as serious offences, the more so when in such a sensitive district. Mr Kimberley Bull, chairman of Oxted Magistrates, when fining a local man the sum of £1 for "showing a light," commented, "We shall not hesitate to send people to prison for a second offence."

Changes were made to improve the aerodrome's security against attack, the Scots Guards becoming a permanent part of the defences and residing in two houses on the north-west fringe of the aerodrome. One, "The Crest," standing next to the north gate, had a high roof on which they made a gun post, setting up a Lewis gun to take advantage of the excellent field of vision. During air raids or moments of tension their colleagues from the barracks were deployed in the wooded areas and commons to the north and west to protect the aerodrome against capture by parachute troops. At night they kept a constant watch on the whole neighbourhood.

August started quietly, then the usual pattern of attacks on convoys and small-scale incursions overland continued until the middle of the month, when the Luftwaffe changed the emphasis. On the twelfth, in common with others along the coast, the Kenley Sector's radar station at Pevensey was bombed, being put out of action for a few hours. The significance of what they had achieved was lost on the Germans, who did not fully realise the importance of the stations to the defence system. Had they known that the British were deprived of their early warning advantage, then no doubt a more thorough job would have been attempted. Perhaps it was thought that enough damage had already been done to put the station out of action permanently; it would seem that once a target of this nature had been bombed it was their policy to cross it off the map.

Forays against radar stations were the harbinger of greater things. The following day had been designated "Eagle Day" by the bumptious Reichsmarschall Goering, the Luftwaffe Commander-in-Chief, and on that day the Germans began to make greater efforts to destroy Fighter Command and soften up the British defences in the hope that favourable conditions could be created for the invasion; or perhaps to force Britain to come to terms.

By this time the population was well accustomed to the air raid siren and most people subconsciously kept an ear cocked for the now familiar rising and falling wail of the "alert" that usually announced the approach of raiders. Often it was a long time before the steady note of the "all clear" released them from the confines of their shelters, sometimes after not having heard any air activity at all.

Unfortunately misjudging of German intentions sometimes led to the warning being sounded too late, as on 15th August, when the aerodrome at Croydon was bombed in the first really big raid in the area. Sixty-three people, mostly civilians working in factories on the fringe of the aerodrome, were killed and many more injured. As their home base burned, the Hurricanes of Squadron-Leader John Thompson's No 111 Squadron took their revenge in the air, and it was a very much depleted German force that picked its way home. It has been suggested that the bombing of Croydon was a mistake by the Germans due to a navigational error, and that they were in fact looking for Kenley. Because of restrictions imposed by Hitler on the bombing of London it was thought that Croydon, being situated in the suburbs, was immune from attack. It is worth remembering, however, that Croydon Airport had a very distinctive appearance and was not at all like Kenley, with its concrete runways and square hangars. It was also a front-line fighter station and in German eyes a perfectly legitimate military target, and they reminded everyone of this three days later when they bombed it again.

There is no question as to whether they had doubts about Croydon being an R.A.F. station. In his book *The Game of the Foxes*, Ladislas Farago tells of the spy Arthur Owens, a Welshman who, while resident at Kingston, Surrey, set up a circle of spies, one of whom is alleged to have watched Kenley. During the period immediately prior to the outbreak of war and for the first few weeks of war Owens, both by radio and personal contact, gave the Germans detailed information about Croydon; the number of Hurricanes there, etc. It is of interest to note that on 22nd October during a meeting in Brussels with an Abwehr (German

The outer structure of a 1917 vintage hangar showing the triple brick columns which supported the sliding doors. The workshops on the side of the building were added several years after the hangar had been built. *Author*

Intelligence) contact, he gave an exact description of the camouflage of the administration building. Four days later, "Lord Haw Haw" (the traitor William Joyce) in a broadcast to Britain from Hamburg,* warned the people of Croydon to evacuate the aerodrome area because it was about to be bombed. The choice of his words is significant. "We not only know the aerodrome is camouflaged, but we know just what kind of camouflage it is." The Messerschmitts on the raid were seen deliberately to overfly Kenley on their way to raid Croydon.

Having changed the direction of its assault, the Luftwaffe concentrated on the systematic destruction of Fighter Command's aerodromes, and any others likely to provide bases from which the R.A.F. could deploy aircraft against an invasion fleet. Noting the latest pattern of attacks against aerodromes, most people realised that it was not so much a question of whether Kenley would be raided as of when.

Sunday, 18th August was warm and sunny with little cloud about. Throughout the morning, aerial activity was light; nothing of importance had occurred to disturb the otherwise typically English summer's day. At 12.45 p.m. Operations Room shifts were changing over, but, noting a high degree of German activity being reported by the coastal radar, senior controller Squadron Leader Norman remained behind with the relief controller, Pilot Officer David Owen-Edmunds, to see what transpired. The threat was beginning to attain sizable proportions and Norman was instructed by group headquarters at Uxbridge to "scramble" No 615 Squadron. Seven Hurricanes led by Joe Kayll took off and were followed almost immediately by five more. Next to go were eight Spitfires of No 64 Squadron under Squadron Leader Aeneas MacDonell.

Local air raid warden Stephen Reid, living in "Langley Marish", a bungalow bordering the aerodrome near the north gate, heard the instruction being given over the aerodrome loudspeaker system to pilots at dispersal, and before the civilian air raid siren was sounded he was already on his rounds telling people nearby to take cover.

Soon after 1 p.m. a large force of nearly sixty enemy aircraft flew over the coast in two waves at medium and high altitude. Their course immediately came under the watchful eye of the Observer Corps, whose attention was also soon attracted to a small force of nine Dornier 17s which had approached Beachy Head at sea level under the radar cover. Led by Hauptmann Joachim Roth, the aircraft of 9 Staffel Kampfgeschwader 76 (a specialist low-level attack unit) began skilfully hedge-hopping their way at little more than fifty feet across country towards their target, Kenley. The final part of their course was to take them over

*Hamburg was also home of the Abwehr branch which specialised in the clandestine coverage of Britain.

Bletchingly to climb the sharply rising ground on the southern side of the North Downs and on over Caterham.

At Croydon, twelve pilots of No 111 Squadron sat strapped in their Hurricanes tensely awaiting instructions from the Kenley Controller. When German intentions became clearer, Red Section, Pilot-Officer Walker and Sergeants Craig and Elkin, with their "A" Flight colleagues of Yellow Section, Sergeants Dymond, Hampshire and Deacon, were "scrambled" at 13.05 hours. Several minutes later "B" Flight, comprising Green Section, Flight Lieutenant Connors, D.F.C., Pilot Officer Simpson and Sergeant Wallace, together with Blue Section, Sergeants Brown, Hardman and Newton, were ordered off and got airborne on a course which conveniently took them in the general direction of the aerodrome at Kenley. Instructions from the ground came to them rapidly and were confusing; in a few seconds they were told to patrol base at 20,000 feet, 5,000 feet then 3,000 feet and finally to intercept a small formation of enemy bombers who were about to attack Kenley at fifty feet.

Mrs Whittaker, wife of the local greengrocer, was playing a game of darts in the back garden of the shop in Caterham High Street when her attention was attracted by the noise of aero engines growing rapidly to

Flying just a few feet above the waves, the Dornier Do.17Z-2s of 9/KG76 are passing Beachy Head and approaching Cuckmere Haven on their way to Kenley on 18th August, 1940. This is one of a remarkable sequence of pictures taken by German photographer Rolf von Rebal, who flew on the low-level mission. *Bundesarchiv*

alarming proportions and causing windows to rattle with the vibration. Looking up, she was shocked to see several German aircraft burst into view, what seemed like a few feet above the rooftops. It appeared as if their arrival above her was a signal for one to open fire and bursts of machine-gun fire added to the already mind-numbing spectacle. Major Marshall was hit in the legs as he stood at the entrance to an air raid shelter on the corner of Park Avenue and Stanstead Road.

Probably the first No 111 Squadron Hurricanes to make contact with the Dorniers came from "A" Flight who, having turned back towards Kenley, had a brush with some of the enemy aircraft before breaking away as they approached the aerodrome defences. Undeterred, the German aircraft continued on over Caterham, spread out and formed into three distinctive groups, each of three aircraft; they were on the most exacting part of their journey, running up to the target.

Mrs Whittaker's husband, a member of the Auxiliary Fire Service, was on duty at the Westway fire station. He was standing on the station forecourt when the raiders appeared over the Caterham rooftops. Instantly realising they were German, he flung himself to the ground as a stream of machine-gun bullets smashed into a row of five ambulances parked nearby, putting them all out of action. Lying on the ground, "more intent on self-preservation than anything else," he was amazed at how clearly he could see the German aircrew in their positions in the aircraft.

From the third floor of St Lawrence's Hospital, Reg Williams looked into the cockpit of the leading Dornier of the westerly group, noting the

Opposite: Hedge-hopping over Balcombe on the way to Kenley: another of Rolf von Rebal's pictures, showing the Balcombe to Haywards Heath road running from left to right with "Yew Tree Cottage", "Fernleigh" with two bay windows, and the old cottage "Troytown" in the centre. *Bundesarchiv*

Right: The Balcombe to Haywards Heath road in 1984. The cottages with their distinctive bay windows and the older cottage in the background can be clearly seen in the centre of Rolf von Rebal's picture. *Author*

steel-helmeted figure of the pilot at the controls as the beautiful green-camouflaged machine flew up Coulsdon Road before turning with its two associates to line up on the aerodrome, one having come from behind the hospital and over Caterham barracks.

From one of the nine aircraft came a few small bombs, badly damaging three cottages in Oak Road and killing Mrs Charlton. Bomb or shell fragments struck Mr Wright, the local Registrar of Births and Deaths, as he stood in Burntwood Lane. The horse pulling Latham's Dairies' milk float was also hit, and died between the shafts.

The good fortune which the Germans had enjoyed as they hedgehopped across country, unruffled by the defences, now ran out. To the Germans' alarm, it immediately became clear when they sighted the aerodrome that the timing of the raid had gone wrong; the main force should already have bombed to soften up the defences, but there was no indication of this. They had no choice but to carry on.

On the aerodrome Pilot Officer Lofts had just finished strapping himself into a Hurricane and was preparing to take off. The men manning ground defences, forewarned and prepared, were carefully watching the southern boundary. However deceptive the low-flying Dorniers had tried to be in their approach, good communications

An oblique aerial photograph of Kenley taken in 1931 showing the aerodrome at top right, with Hayes Lane running left to right and Old Lodge Lane winding along from bottom left to join Hayes Lane in the centre of the picture. At the outbreak of the Second World War the road was blocked at the right-hand edge of the picture and the large white house nearby, "The Crest", was used as a gunpost; it was destroyed by a bomb on 18th August, 1940. One of the low-level raiders was brought down at the far end of Golf Road, top left. *Surrey County Libraries*

between Observer Corps posts had enabled an accurate picture to be plotted of their course, and their destination was obvious.

By a fine piece of navigation, Joachim Roth had brought his nine aircraft up to the target. Without the advantage of height, when landmarks appear at a leisurely pace, the course had been difficult to accomplish. Pilots now lined up their aircraft on previously selected parts of the aerodrome. As the leading Dornier approached the aerodrome boundary, Pilot Officer Lofts was speeding along the runway and getting airborne on a converging course which would take him directly into its path. A collision was averted by Lofts pulling the Hurricane round in a sharp right turn; whether this was a deliberate manoeuvre to get out of the way or he was oblivious to the danger must remain a matter for conjecture.

At No 615 Squadron dispersal on the Whyteleafe side of the aerodrome, Gene Roux stood at the entrance to an air raid shelter, leaving it to the last moment before taking cover. As the bombers came roaring in, he watched the leading aircraft's bombs go down into the hangars. Suddenly he became aware of pieces of brick chipping off and flying from the shelter entrance beside him. Not wishing to remain the number one attraction for a German machine-gunner, he hastily launched himself into the shelter.

The bombs used were fitted with special fuses which allowed a small time lapse before detonating to enable the low-flying aircraft to get clear. The leading aircraft released its bombs safely, but the one following took an enormous blast as the leader's bombs exploded underneath it. Eyewitnesses were astounded to see it lurch upwards in an alarming manner, yet still remain airborne.

With very little time lapse between them the three Dornier groups, each on a slightly different course taking them over their pre-selected area of the aerodrome, poured their lethal loads into the hangars and buildings, across taxiways, runways and dispersal bays. With machine-gun and 20 mm cannon they shot at any worthwhile targets.

Bombs falling on to the hangars met with little resistance, the hangar roofs being constructed almost entirely of wood and ripe for combustion. In a trice, three of the hangars were blown to pieces and engulfed by fire. At a gunpost high up on the door support of the old No 7 hangar, R.A.F. gunner Corporal Storry continued firing his Lewis gun even when the building beneath him was crumbling away. More bombs exploded on the hospital block and around the shelter where the hospital staff had sought refuge.

Most of the aircraft, still maintaining minimum height, continued across the aerodrome, which by now had taken on the appearance of a battlefield. Bombs were exploding everywhere, punctuating a continuous background of noise from machine-guns, cannon, Bofors and other guns. The defenders were hitting back, pouring streams of fire from all directions at the raiders.

Pilots of the three leading aircraft in the middle section received a shock as they approached the northern boundary. Unexpectedly, a line of rockets shot into the air in front of them, each dragging a steel cable into the path of the oncoming aircraft. The leader somehow squeezed through, although it is thought that he touched a cable. One of the other Dorniers in the group was less fortunate, receiving the full effect as a wing made contact. Instinctively the pilot, thought to be Feldwebel Wilhelm Raab, took evasive action, fighting the drag imposed on the wing. As the aircraft flew on A.C.2 H. W. Knowles, the Parachute and Cable operator, watched it disappear low down in the direction of Whyteleafe with the parachutes trailing behind; the cable came off and the machine survived.

Near the north gate the Scots Guards were occupying "The Crest", a large private house, as their detachment headquarters. Being almost on the aerodrome, which allowed a good view, the Guards had a Lewis gun mounted on its high roof. The three Dorniers of the westerly attacking group continued across the aerodrome and were being heavily engaged by the ground defences. On the roof of "The Crest" the gunner, possibly Lance-Corporal J. Miller, kept his gun in action even at point blank range. Taking careful aim, and with perfect timing, a bomb aimer in one of the Dorniers settled the almost eyeball to eyeball confrontation. As his aircraft skimmed the roof he released a bomb which reduced the house to rubble, silencing the gun. One of the Dorniers in the group, riddled with bullets, staggered on and struck one of the Parachutes and Cables released by A.C.2 D. Roberts before colliding with a tree and breaking up, the major part falling on to a bungalow at the far end of Golf Road and catching fire, the rest disintegrating and hurtling through the air for a further seventy yards before coming to rest in a field.*

Down in Whyteleafe Valley, young Peter Skegg and his father were walking their district on A.R.P. duty when they heard the sound of gunfire and explosions coming from the direction of Kenley. This rapidly became overwhelmed by the sound of aero engines from approaching low-flying aircraft; above the trees the unmistakable shape of a Dornier burst into view, closely followed by two others.

From above, two Hurricane pilots of No 111 Squadron's "B" Flight, which had just taken off from Croydon, spotted the fleeing German aircraft and, executing a half roll, turned and dived down to attack.

*See Appendix five.

Looking out over the port engine of one of the Dornier Do.17s of the low-level raiding group as it is about to clear the northern boundary of the aerodrome. Above the No 64 Squadron Spitfire in the blast pen can be seen clouds of dust rising as another Dornier engages a gunpost near the North gate, and beyond that can be seen Hayes Lane snaking away at top left. Very soon the house with the tall chimneys at top right, "The Crest", which supports a Scots Guards gunpost, will come under attack and be destroyed. Continuing its course, the photographer's aircraft will pass close to the spot where Petersen's Dornier will crash in Golf Road. *Bundesarchiv*

From their exposed position in Valley Road, a little more than half a mile from the aerodrome, Peter and his father watched the Hurricanes curving down to attack the Dorniers from the rear. The leading Hurricane took on the second bomber while his colleague settled for the third and had already opened fire from an almost vertical position on the way down. His bullets began to strike the ground uncomfortably close to the watching pair, who were lying flat on the road. To them what was in fact just a few moments seemed to be an age, almost as if the whole scene was being enacted in slow motion. The combatants dipped down into Whyteleafe Valley and disappeared from sight up over Riddlesdown, one German aircraft apparently trailing smoke.

As the remaining eight Dorniers made for home in varying stages of disarray, No 111 Squadron's Hurricanes remained in hot pursuit intent on revenge.

At Kenley, as soon as the noise died down, people started to emerge from their shelters to take stock of the damage. The remains of three hangars were being rapidly consumed by fire and thick black smoke was being blown across the aerodrome by a south-westerly breeze. A number of other ancillary buildings had been damaged or destroyed, including the hospital block, which was also on fire.

At "The Crest" three Guardsmen and their Commanding Officer, Second Lieutenant James Hague, were trapped in the debris of the fallen

Smoke from the fires on Kenley aerodrome after the raid of 18th August, 1940, seen from behind St Andrew's Church, Coulsdon, two miles to the north-west. The peaceful appearance of the view over Coulsdon to the right of the church is deceptive, as reports in the Incident Book of Coulsdon and Purley Council reveal:

    13.15 1 dead Chipstead Valley Road, Brighton Road junction.
    13.15 10 casualties Malcolm Road, junction with Woodcote Grove Road.
    14.05 Bomb at *Red Lion* exploded.

One of the casualties caused by the Malcolm Road bomb also died. These bombs came from the high-altitude raiders, who presumably aimed them at the railway. Houses in Malcolm Road are seen immediately to the right of the church, with the mock-Tudor *Red Lion* public house above. Chipstead Valley Road joins Brighton road opposite the *Red Lion*.

building. After being dug out from the rubble, Second Lieutenant Hague set about organising his men and moving them to safety. Although in great pain from a crushed shoulder, he led them and their colleagues from a nearby slit trench (which was threatened by a burning petrol bowser) out into the open to a safer place. Lance-Corporal John Gale had been blown up by a bomb falling near his slit trench but still went to the aid of the men trapped at "The Crest" and courageously carried an injured Guardsman on his back to safety, although he was himself hurt, with two broken ribs.

It was while the men were scurrying across the open ground that the main German bomber force arrived overhead and released their loads from high altitude. To create a terrorising effect, their bombs were fitted with small paper tubes pierced with holes through which air was forced as the bomb fell, making a spine-chilling scream.

Smoke and flames from the Kenley fires clearly indicated to the twelve leading Junkers Ju.88 aircrews that something had gone amiss with the timing of the raid; they were to have been the first to arrive, supposedly to dive-bomb from high altitude. The next to attack were to have been twenty-seven Dornier 17s bombing from high altitude, and it was after them, five minutes later, that the low-flying nine should have appeared. The purpose of the Ju.88s' participation in the raid had already been achieved, making their effort superfluous, so the pilots turned away to look for Manston, their alternative target. It was the high-flying Dorniers that were now showering Kenley and the surrounding district with bombs. One or two aircraft overflew Kenley and continued on to Croydon to drop a few bombs on the aerodrome there before turning and joining their colleagues on the homeward journey.

As the drone of aircraft engines died away, the sound of church bells could be heard coming from somewhere in the district. This was the recognised warning that the invasion had started; someone had mistakenly thought parachutes seen descending over Kenley were part of a German assault force. They were in fact supporting 480-foot lengths of steel cable, part of the aerodrome P.A.C. defences.

Air Raid Warden Stephen Reid had almost reached the security of the wardens' post in Old Lodge Lane when the bombs started to fall. With his colleague, Mr Robbins, he was caught out in the open at the junction of Hayes Lane and Old Lodge Lane. Clinging to the trembling ground as the bombs detonated a few yards away, they witnessed from very close at hand the duel between the Dornier and the Guardsmen at "The Crest". Not ten yards away a pair of semi-detached bungalows was hit, one of them being almost totally wrecked, while its neighbour strangely received only very minor damage. Picking themselves up, they went about their duty, checking on damage to property and seeing to the wellbeing of the people.

Stephen Reid said later:

A thick haze of chalk dust filled the air like fog. We became aware of a lone figure marching down the road towards us. As he got closer we recognised him as one of the local firemen, but the strange thing was, he was wearing a gas mask. We later discovered the reason for this odd behaviour. He sheepishly admitted to having thought the dust cloud was poison gas. Even he could see the funny side of it and roared with laughter.

When we got down to the end of Golf Road, we saw the wreckage of a Dornier lying on top of "Sunnycroft", a detached bungalow. On top of the heap, which was now burning fiercely, a German airman was trying to extricate himself from the wreckage. I noticed that one of his arms was missing; it seemed that he must have been trying to get out while the aircraft was still in the air before it crashed, because we later found his arm several yards away in a field. It was still enclosed in the sleeve of his uniform. There was little we could do for him or his colleagues and they all perished in the fire.

The workings of the human mind in times of stress are sometimes odd. With that horrifying scene in front of me, unexploded bombs, bullets exploding in the heat of the fire, etc., the thing which registered most clearly in my mind was that the German's boot had a large hole worn in the sole, and I remember thinking, "You think you are the master race, yet you wear worn-out boots." This silly little thing somehow seemed important at the time.

"Sunnycroft" was occupied by Mrs Turner-Smith and Mr Shackerby, who had three guests to lunch. When the aircraft crashed on to the bungalow it trapped them all inside. By good fortune one of the hallway walls stood firm while the other gave way and leaned on to it forming a small tunnel through which they were able to crawl to safety. They were obviously all badly shaken but fortunately unharmed. We decided to send Mrs Turner-Smith to hospital for a check-up; she was getting on in years and the shock could have had a bad effect later on.

By an odd twist of fate, she was the owner of "The Crest," which had been requisitioned by the Army and used as a gunpost which, just a few seconds earlier, had also been destroyed.

Mrs Hilda Marshal was still in her "dugout" when we arrived at "Highleigh". A bomb had penetrated the garden fence and failed to explode. It was resting a yard from the entrance to the shelter. Hilda was a remarkable old lady; she came out and stepped over it without turning a hair.

From his vantage point on the opposite side of the valley at Whyteleafe, half way up Tithe Pit Shaw Lane, James Bull had watched the first bombs fall on Kenley. As the bullets started to fly, he made a dash for a nearby public air raid shelter. From inside, the sounds of the battle going on overhead filtered in with alarming clarity. When the occupants emerged later, their eyes squinting in the bright sunlight, it was to Kenley that they looked. Of the aerodrome little could be seen through a great cloud of smoke which was being blown across by the light south-west wind. Close by in a field on Batts Farm several cows lay dead, victims of stray machine-gun bullets.

A number of people out in the open were machine-gunned, probably by friend and foe alike, each intent on the destruction of the other. At West Wickham a Dornier lost an engine which fell into a private garden, and nearby a rubber boat also fell out of the aircraft. Where the German aircraft came from and its eventual fate remains unknown.

Still flying at treetop height, the remaining eight Dorniers of Kampfgeschwader 76 scattered far and wide in a desperate struggle for survival. Damage received at Kenley and repeated attacks by No 111 Squadron's Hurricanes were taking their toll.

One Dornier finally succumbed in a field of stubble at Leaves Green, near Biggin Hill. Two more got as far as the English Channel before their

The crashed Dornier Do.17 of the leader of the low-level attack on Kenley, Hauptmann Joachim Roth, in a field at Leaves Green, near Biggin Hill, guarded by two armed soldiers.   *Imperial War Museum*

damaged engines could no longer support them and they fell into the water.

Their opponents were also suffering heavily. Flight Lieutenant Connors, leading No 111 Squadron, had plunged into the attack, closely followed by his number two, Pilot Officer Peter Simpson, the two Hurricanes engaging the German aircraft from close range. Unable to slow down to match their speed with that of the slower Dorniers, they got in as many bursts of fire as possible before breaking away to avoid a collision. Connors was seen to detach himself safely, but his aircraft was later seen falling in flames and he died in the ensuing crash. After seeing smoke coming from one engine of his adversary, Peter Simpson was forced to break away upwards as there was insufficient height to do anything else; this left the underside of his Hurricane exposed and presenting an opportunity of which a German air gunner was quick to take advantage.

Group Captain Peter Simpson, D.S.O., D.F.C., R.A.F. Rtd. writes:

> There were extremely loud bangs and a terrific thud, bits and pieces of metal began to fly about the cockpit. My right foot felt as if it had fallen off. The R/T had gone dead and the aircraft's controls felt very sloppy, so I decided to climb to a safe height with the intention of jumping out. I undid my harness, pushed back the hood and was about to turn the aircraft on to its back when I looked down and noticed a bright blue swimming pool glistening in the sunlight; my attention was further attracted to it by the figure of a girl in a white bathing costume lounging at the side of the pool.
>
> Into view came a golf course and I instantly decided to try to put the Hurricane down on the practice fairway; the course itself appeared to have anti-parachutist wires strung across it. This I successfully did.
>
> After switching off everything in case of fire I stepped down from the aircraft, and immediately the pain from my injured foot became intense. Two golfers appeared and, with their clubs raised above their heads, they advanced menacingly towards me, intent on making me their prisoner. I told them I was English and, in an inspired moment, pulled out a packet of Players to prove it. They helped me to the clubhouse where I was treated like royalty. A doctor was called and after he had removed my boot and sock, he gave my foot a bit of a tug and placed a fairly large piece of metal in my hand. There were still several small pieces left in my foot, but it was all right.
>
> I learned that I was at the Woodcote Park Golf Course near Epsom (now the R.A.C. Country Club).
>
> After several fruitless attempts to get through to Croydon on the telephone,* and a word with Inspector Jeffs of the Epsom Police, one of the members drove me back to Croydon.

Experiences of his colleagues as they pursued the fleeing raiders on their homeward journey were varied. Yellow Section's leaders, Sergeants Dymond and Brown, watched the occupants of their Leaves Green victim running for shelter in a wood. Yellow three, Sergeant Deacon's Hurricane, was believed to have been shot down in error by A.A. fire after destroying a Ju.88. Sergeant Craig was the only one of Red Section to make contact with the enemy when he tangled with a Dornier which he later claimed as a "probable." His colleagues in Red Section failed to pick out the German aircraft against the background of fields and trees.

Blue three, Sergeant Harry Newton, had recently celebrated his twentieth birthday. He was still very inexperienced; in fact it required all his concentration and effort just to stay in formation with the rest of the

---

*Unknown to him, before he arrived back the usual official telegram had already been sent to his mother reporting him "missing". It was not until his brother arrived at Croydon some time later to make inquiries about Peter that the telegram affair came to light.

squadron. After "scrambling" from Croydon, he soon became detached as the squadron split up in the rush to get to grips with the Dorniers. While alone over Kenley, he looked down and for the very first time saw bombs exploding beneath him. He also saw one of the Dorniers that had bombed earlier sneaking off home, trying not to attract attention as it skimmed above the treetops. Although lacking in experience, he was not lacking in courage or determination, and this first sight of bombs falling on English soil triggered off a sense of blind fury within him. Diving down on to his prey, he pushed back the Hurricane's hood, immediately losing his maps and charts in the great rush of air, and switched the gun button to "fire". Bullets from both aircraft struck home, those of the German gunner initially having the greater effect. Harry Newton's aircraft burst into flames and it became crucial to his survival that he should gain sufficient height to be able to bale out. He came down by parachute near Tatsfield Beacon, his face and hands badly burned, a few yards away from the wreckage of his Hurricane.

Squadron Leader Joe Kayll's Hurricanes were also having a tough time. At the outset No 615 Squadron's instructions were to take on the fighter escort of the high-flying bombers, and in so doing they became widely scattered. Most successful pilot was Flight Lieutenant Sanders, who claimed to have shot down a Heinkel He.111 from which four crewmen baled out before it crashed south of Kenley. He also managed later to get among a bunch of Ju.88s over Kent and claimed one shot down near Westerham. He was not yet finished; together with another Hurricane, he despatched another Ju.88 near Sevenoaks, in the same area that Squadron Leader Joe Kayll's victim, an Me.109, was last seen heading earthwards with smoke pouring from it. Pilot Officers Young, McClintock and Lofts each had non-conclusive engagements with Dorniers. Lofts sat filled with frustration as he watched his victim limp out to sea with one engine stopped; he had run out of ammunition. Flight Lieutenant Giddings and Flying Officer Gray also damaged enemy aircraft. On the debit side, pilots Gaunce, Looker and Hugo each suffered misfortunes. Flight Lieutenant Gaunce baled out of his blazing machine after an encounter with an Me.109; Pilot Officers Hugo and Looker also fell foul of the Me.109 escort and made emergency landings. They were admitted to Orpington and Croydon Hospitals respectively.

Twenty-year-old Sergeant Walley became involved in a ferocious dog fight over Worcester Park and received serious damage to his aircraft. Rather than bale out, he stayed in it and tried to make a forced landing in Morden Park. On the last few yards of his approach, the crippled Hurricane came in too low and Walley had to pull it up to clear some private houses. On reaching the park, things went wrong, the machine struck some trees and he died in the burning wreckage of his aircraft.*

From over 20,000 feet above Kenley, the eight Spitfire pilots of Aeneas MacDonell's No 64 Squadron had watched the first bombs fall on the aerodrome. Diving down too late to intervene, they climbed back up to intercept the high-level raiders as they turned for home. On their return, No 64 Squadron's weary pilots claimed a mixed bag of Dornier, Messerschmitt, Ju.88 and Heinkel either damaged or unconfirmed victories.

At the height of the raid men and girls in the Operations building stayed resolutely at their posts, expecting at any moment to see the flimsy building fall about them. Protection afforded by the earth wall surrounding the building was minimal, and even a few well-aimed cannon shells would have proved disastrous. It was not of a construction that inspired confidence in anyone under attack, and it could well have been the camouflage netting draped over the top, shielding it from German eyes, that contributed most to the safety of the occupants. No one, when the building was designed and constructed in 1924, could have envisaged the treatment the structure was subjected to that day in 1940. When the ground beneath them stopped heaving from the effects of the explosions and the shower of debris ceased raining down upon the roof, the duty watch began to relax a little.

A quick check revealed that all telephone lines except one were dead. Their only link with the outside world was through a line to Bromley Observer Corps Centre. Almost all effective control in the Sector was now gone, but this one line enabled contact to be maintained with other control centres.

Controller Owen-Edmunds called everyone together to speak to them. "You have all been bloody marvellous," he said. "I think the Germans will soon return to finish us off and when they do, I hope you will continue to face it in the manner you have just shown."

Outside, people felt it safe to start moving about again. Emerging from their shelters, airmen and W.A.A.F.s were shocked to see the devastation. A great column of thick black smoke from the burning hangars was rising many thousands of feet into the air. The crackling of

*In 1971 Merton Technical College was built on the spot where Walley crashed in Morden Park; today's young people, much the same age as he was when he died, now shape their future life there. Local people did not forget him and they had a plaque placed on the wall of the college. It is inscribed as follows:
"Plaque erected by public subscription to honour the memory of No. 819018 Sergeant P. K. Walley, Battle of Britain pilot of 615 Squadron, Royal Auxiliary Air Force, 20 years old. Shot down by enemy raiders August 18th 1940. It is recalled with pride that, knowing he was about to crash, Sergeant Walley bravely managed to guide his badly damaged aircraft over nearby houses. Thereby safeguarding the lives of the residents."

the fires was punctuated by an occasional explosion as bombs continued to detonate. From above, the sound of aircraft and gunfire could still be heard. Wrecked aircraft and motor transport were liberally scattered around the airfield; the German airmen had been pretty thorough.

Men began feverishly digging away the earth and debris to free their colleagues entombed in No 13 Air Raid Shelter, close to the burning hospital block. As if by some evil design, bombs had fallen each end of the crescent-shaped shelter, effectively sealing it off. Most of those who died were buried at the entrances, but further in people were still alive. One of the first to get to the shelter was Corporal Fred Jenner, who had nothing to dig with except his hands. A few shovels were found and put to use by the toiling men, who eventually cleared a way into the centre section and carefully helped the occupants out. W.A.A.F. Mary Coulthard had received a wound to her thigh, thought to have been caused by the damaged edge of a steel helmet. Seeing that she might be in need of a little help, Fred Jenner walked over to her, quietly explaining that there was nothing to feel embarrassed about; "I am a married man," he told her.

Among the fatalities was No 615 Squadron Medical Officer, Flight Lieutenant Crombie, whose death was felt as a deep personal loss by many who knew him either socially or by having been in his professional care; it was a feeling which extended beyond the aerodrome into many local homes, for before joining up he had been the local general practitioner. Out at dispersal Leading Aircraftman Holroyd was dead,

The Hawker Hurricane of No 615 Squadron flown by Pilot Officer Looker which made a forced landing at Croydon on 18th August, 1940. It is now preserved and on permanent display at the Science Museum at South Kensington.   *Science Museum, London*

killed by shrapnel. Another No 615 Squadron man, Leading Aircraftman Turner, was carefully removed from the cab of a lorry, suffering from shrapnel wounds, from which he died in Purley Hospital the following day. Other people's injuries were treated as well as possible until outside help came. The Station's medical supplies were in the burning ruin which a few minutes earlier had been the hospital.

Kenley's fighters, low on fuel and ammunition, either diverted to other airfields or found a reasonably safe strip on which to land among the bomb craters. When Joe Kayll landed at Redhill he was struck by a marked lack of welcome. Nothing stirred, he recalled. "I well remember that I had the greatest difficulty in getting refuelled as everyone there had been ordered into shelters or slit trenches; it required some pretty strong words to get them out to fill up my Hurricane."

Pilot Officer Looker received a very hot reception when he brought his damaged aircraft in to land at Croydon. Jittery gunners of the airfield defences opened up on the crippled aircraft, fortunately with little effect.* Sergeant Craig of No 111 Squadron circled Croydon waiting for the furore caused by the raid to die down before landing.

Some of the aerodrome's fire appliances were damaged, leaving the fire section with its already meagre resources further depleted; even at full strength the task before the section's personnel would have been insurmountable. A call for assistance went out to the district, and local fire brigades were soon on the scene. One of the first fire crews to arrive was from the Westway station at Caterham who were directed to try to control the fire which was greedily engulfing the hospital block near the hangars.

W. J. Carey drove one of the Purley brigade's engines up Old Lodge Lane and through the gap where once the North Gate had stood. He carefully picked his way around bomb craters, wrecked vehicles and shattered aircraft to get to the fires raging on the other side. He noted how accurate German cannon and machine-gun fire had been, particularly when dealing with the aircraft. The Purley brigade was also set to work on the hospital block; by that time any hope of salvaging anything of the hangars was gone. As they were running out the hoses, an exploding oxygen cylinder hurtled through the air from one of the burning hangars and smashed into the side of the fire engine. The firemen were further hampered by a burning petrol bowser which was expected to blow up at any moment. To the firemen's profound admiration, a soldier drove up to it in a lorry and, with little regard for his own safety, hitched a heavy chain to the front of the burning vehicle and towed it clear. Initially there was a shortage of water due to a bomb

*This Hurricane was later restored and is now on permanent display at the Science Museum, London.

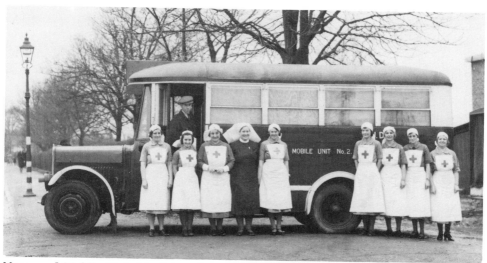

Nurses of Mobile Unit No 2 based at Westway, Caterham, one of those which gave assistance on the aerodrome after the air raid of 18th August, 1940. *Surrey County Libraries*

fracturing the water main down in Whyteleafe, but relays of pumps were connected up to pipe water up to the aerodrome from the valley and elsewhere.

Reports of parachutists descending on Kenley very soon created a feeling of nervousness throughout the district as police and the Home Guard rushed to set up road blocks and checkpoints, hampering and restricting the movement of both civilians and the rescue services. Canadian soldiers riding motor-cycles fitted with sidecars, heavily armed with Lewis guns, called at the A.R.P. post in Valley Road to inquire whether the Wardens there had seen any shot-down German airmen or parachutes descending in the area. After receiving a negative reply, they moved briskly off to search the woodlands to the north. Anyone falling into their hands was in for a very rough time.

Mobile Emergency Units began arriving in large numbers, some from as far away as Guildford, all guided to the scene by the pall of smoke rising over Kenley. Soon the access roads became so choked with vehicles that essential aid was delayed in getting through. When a call for medical assistance was sent out to local doctors, Dr Lewis, the district's Senior Medical Officer, drove to the aerodrome as quickly as possible. Seeing the congestion in the roads ahead, he prudently parked his car and walked the rest of the way. He set up a medical post in the remaining

The front of the Officers' Mess at Kenley showing repairs to the damage caused in the air raid of 18th August, 1940. *Author*

hangar, treating mostly burns. Lodged in the gutter of the roof above, an unexploded bomb rested unobserved. Such bombs had been detonating at infrequent intervals while rescue work was in progress.

Just before the attack, a party of W.A.A.F.s was about to be transported by coach to the emergency Operations Room in Caterham. Word was now sent round for those available to proceed there as best they could. Other than a telephone link, there was little that could be done from there; it was not operational and was only used for training W.A.A.F.s in Operations Room work.

Order steadily gained strength over the earlier chaos and by late afternoon a safe landing strip had been marked out in brightly coloured tape among the bomb craters, enabling the rest of the fighters to return from satellite aerodromes. Pilot Officer Mudie of No 615 Squadron had experienced difficulty earlier, running into a bomb crater. Afternoon tea was prepared and then postponed when another attack alarm sent everyone scurrying to the shelters.

Royal Engineers bomb disposal teams scoured the area for unexploded bombs; they were not disappointed. Of the hundred or so bombs that had fallen on the target, twenty-five had failed to detonate, twelve of them later being rendered harmless. The others were moved to a safe place for future attention. The one in the hangar gutter was left there overnight while disposal men considered the best method of removing it.

Damage caused by exploding bombs had dramatically transformed the Station scene. One hangar remained; where the other three had once stood was only a series of brick walls and support arches standing among the twisted wreckage of burned motor-cars and aircraft. Station headquarters and the camp hospital were mere rubble, and barrack blocks and the Sergeants' Mess had also been hit. The Officers' Mess had escaped comparatively unscathed, with only superficial damage from bomb splinters to the front of the building. It appeared as if the whole of the area had been liberally sprayed with machine-gun bullets; this was not confined solely to the aerodrome, much damage to property being in evidence to the south at Caterham.

Ten aircraft, six of them Hurricanes of No 615 Squadron, were destroyed or damaged beyond repair and six more, including a Spitfire and two Hurricanes, were damaged. A heavy loss in motor transport had also been incurred, the remains of vehicles being much in evidence around the aerodrome. Considering the severity of the bombardment, casualties among personnel were surprisingly light. One officer and eight R.A.F. men were killed; eight others including a W.A.A.F. were injured. A private of 12(HD) Queen's Royal Regiment was severely wounded and died next day; two men from 43rd Light Anti-Aircraft Regiment were minor casualties.

Of the nine low-flying Dorniers which had inflicted the lion's share of the damage, four failed to return to France and two crash landed on reaching friendly soil. While over Kenley the pilot of another aircraft was hit in the chest and collapsed dying in his seat. The navigator, Wilhelm-Friedrich Illg, with great presence of mind, leaned over and took the control column to prevent the aircraft from diving into the ground and successfully held it steady while his colleagues struggled to remove the pilot. They flew on over the eastern suburbs of London and Plumstead Marshes before Illg could take control and turn back for home and a safe landing at St Omer. He had never flown an aircraft before. The other two Dorniers landed at airfields away from their home base before returning; a large number of bullet holes bore witness to the ordeal they had endured. One can imagine the great shock and concern experienced by waiting groundstaff at Cormeilles-en-Vexin when the entire strength of 9 Staffel became overdue; the small comfort when only two aircraft eventually landed back.

That evening the Kenley Sector was so short of serviceable aircraft that it was necessary to ring aerodromes elsewhere to scratch together enough for the dusk patrol over Hawkinge.

When fading light brought the eventful day to a close the men were released and found their way to their favourite haunts in the surrounding district. The W.A.A.F.s, on the other hand, were sent to bed "in case of any nervous reaction." Some were a little peeved. Had they not withstood the stresses of the day equally as well as the men? There had been no panic or hysterical screaming among the company of over one hundred and fifty girls. For young people of both sexes it was a day when, for the first time, they had faced death. For some, it was a moment of truth. When reflecting on the terrors of the previous few hours in the quiet of the evening, they realised that they had stood up to the ordeal remarkably well, and from it gained moral strength.

For the German aircrews of 9 Staffel, Kampfgeschwader 76, it had been a terrible day. Their attack on Kenley had achieved everything they had set out to do, and more. They had made any further bombing of the target by the high-altitude force seem almost superfluous. But what had they really achieved for such a high price in men and machines? Three hangars were destroyed; but these were mostly surplus to requirements, and in fact one was nothing more than a large garage housing private cars owned by Station personnel. Several aircraft were destroyed on the ground; but there were sufficient Hurricanes and Spitfires in reserve to make good the losses overnight. Damaged ancillary buildings were either abandoned in favour of different accommodation or quickly repaired, as were the runways. The most vital building on the aerodrome, the Operations Block, had been missed, through no fault of the aircrews; they simply did not know that it existed. If they had had prior knowledge, with their skilful shooting and bombing tactics it should have been possible to knock it out or at least damage it severely. It must be remembered that the Operations Room was one of the few places the visiting German Air Mission in 1939 was not allowed to see. If they had seen it, perhaps the outcome of the raid would have made the exercise really worthwhile.

The following day was very much "business as usual." Runways were repaired by men of the Royal Engineers, who filled the craters with rubble which had been dumped around the aerodrome for just such a contingency. Their colleagues continued to deal with unexploded bombs.

In a field outside the northern boundary they dug a large pit in which several of the more dangerous examples were detonated. Engineers from the G.P.O. soon repaired damaged telephone lines and the Operations Room resumed normal control of the Sector's fighter strength.

Since the battles to defend the beaches at Dunkirk in May, No 64 Squadron had carried on doggedly in spite of a steady loss of men and machines. Their depleted numbers had been bolstered by an influx of experienced pilots on loan from other squadrons. Peter Simpson of No 111 Squadron had left them a few days earlier after being with them for a fortnight.* The strain of many weeks of air fighting, much of it over the sea where, if you were shot down, your chances of survival were greatly reduced, added extra stress to an already difficult occupation. At this time their principal adversary was fighters whose pilots were full of confidence gained from their earlier success on the Continent. Now battle-weary and very tired, No 64 Squadron was withdrawn to Leconfield to rest.

Three Scots Guardsmen were decorated for bravery during the raid of 18th August. Second Lieutenant J. D. K. Hague received the Military Cross, with Lance-Corporals J. Gale and J. Miller each being awarded the Military Medal. These were the first Scots Guardsmen ever to win medals for gallantry while under fire in the British Isles.

The state of the aerodrome, with its burned out and wrecked motor transport scattered everywhere and bomb craters in abundance, caused a few raised eyebrows among the newly arrived No 616 Squadron Spitfire pilots. Very soon they would be engrossed in their own desperate fight for survival.

Bomb damage in the surrounding district, caused in the main by the high-flying raiders, was widely spread; over one hundred and fifty bombs had missed the target or had been aimed at local railway lines. A very high percentage failed to explode, causing disruption to rail and road services. A number of houses in Caterham and Whyteleafe were demolished or rendered only fit for demolition, others were extensively damaged but repairable. Minor damage to property was considerable with glass and roofs, not surprisingly, suffering badly.

Valley Road was impassable. One house was completely demolished and another badly damaged. In the middle of the road a small hole, little more than twelve inches in diameter, indicated the entry point of an unexploded bomb. The hole remained under the casual observation of Peter Skegg for several days, until one day he noticed that it had become

---

*His conversion from Hurricane to Spitfire is worth recording. "I had to take off, do a circuit and land. Take off again, do a few aerobatics and land once more. From that moment I was put on 'readiness' with the Squadron."

the scene of much activity. Having the natural inquisitiveness of a fifteen-year-old, he quietly wandered up to what was now a very large hole indeed. Peering down into it, he was surprised to see a soldier sitting at the bottom, drinking a cup of tea. His surprise was further enhanced when he realised that the largish lump of metal on which the man was carefully perched was in fact the bomb.

Visits from the Duke of Kent and Mr Winston Churchill did much for morale during this difficult period. During the raid, Parachute and Cable weapons were used for the first time on an aerodrome and this rekindled the interest of the Prime Minister.* One was fired to demonstrate to him the capability of the device. His unheralded arrival with his wife during the evening of 22nd August unfortunately occurred after No 615 Squadron pilots had been released, and they missed the opportunity of meeting their Honorary Air Commodore.

Earlier in the day the bodies of the five German crew members taken from the Golf Road Dornier had been interred at Bandon Hill Cemetery, Beddington. On the lid of each coffin the words "Nazi Airman" was inscribed.

Squadron Leader John Thompson led No 111 Squadron away from Croydon on the same day as their No 64 Squadron colleagues left Kenley. They were withdrawn to Debden, supposedly to rest, but still continued to be brought into action. Taking over at Croydon, Squadron Leader Peter Townsend, with No 85 Squadron, enjoyed a few days of reduced activity, but by the end of a fortnight fourteen of the original eighteen pilots had been shot down and Squadron Leader Townsend was in Croydon General Hospital with a bad foot wound, the result of a clash with an Me.110 over Kent. Such a high rate of attrition could not be endured and on 2nd September they once more changed places with No 111 Squadron, who held the fort with the Spitfires of No 72 Squadron at Croydon until relieved by No 605 Squadron five days later. But this was all in the future.

*See Appendix five.

CHAPTER FIVE

The Achilles Heel

A T KENLEY and Croydon, the few days of inclement weather after the raid had given a welcome respite, the time being devoted to reparation and preparation. When the large-scale concentrated raids were resumed during the latter part of August, losses on both sides were to mount accordingly.

To add to Fighter Command's problems, the Luftwaffe began bombing at night, attacking major towns and cities, including London. This latest extension of the air war at last found the British defence's Achilles Heel. With the Observer Corps blind during the hours of darkness and relying mostly on their hearing, accurate plotting of hostile aircraft once they had flown behind the coastal radar was impossible and a very dangerous situation arose. Even if it had been possible to guide a day fighter to within range of an enemy aircraft, there was no guarantee that its pilot would be able to see it in the dark. A primitive system using experienced day pilots who individually took off and patrolled the night sky, relying mainly on their own instincts to make contact, became the Sector's only form of retaliation apart from the anti-aircraft guns. Success under such circumstances was rare and when Flight Lieutenant Sanders (No 615 Squadron) shot down a Junkers Ju.88* and damaged another near Hastings on the night of 24/25th August, it was acclaimed all the way up to Keith Park, the Group Commander.

Any pleasure gained from the events of that night quickly became forgotten when, on the 26th, No 616 Squadron lost seven Spitfires in a few minutes to Messerschmitt Bf.109s during a clash over the Dover/Deal area; two of the pilots were dead and three wounded. Their colleagues of No 615 Squadron fared no better when later they had four Hurricanes shot down; from these, three of the pilots were wounded. Most of them, like their Spitfire friends, fell to the guns of Messerschmitt Bf.109s over the Kent Coast. The only consolation was the demise of two of their adversaries.

At the end of the month Squadron Leader Kayll took a very tired and battle-weary No 615 Squadron out of the front line to rest and train

---

*Now thought to be a Heinkel He.111 which fell into the sea a mile offshore at 1.30 a.m.

at Prestwick;* that they remained so long in 11 Group, and prior to that had survived the demoralising onslaught in France, must surely be attributed to the high quality of Joe Kayll's leadership.

Thirty-two-year-old Tom Gleave's age did not prevent him from remaining on the flying strength of No 253 Squadron when they moved south from Prestwick under Harold Starr. Tom Gleave being a friend and equal in rank to Starr, the running of the squadron had developed more or less as a partnership between the two men; a partnership which, sadly, fate had decreed was not to last.

On their first day at Kenley Tom Gleave had something of a field day. Finding himself with two of his colleagues in the vicinity of a large formation of Messerschmitt Bf.109s, he carefully manoeuvred into position and selected his first victim. Three of them felt the effects of his guns and departed from the formation in various states of distress before the attentions of their colleagues forced him to break off. By the time the day's flying was over, two of his colleagues were dead, one was missing and another wounded. The following day, Gleave's good fortune deserted him. While leading seven Hurricanes against a raid to the south-east of Kenley, his aircraft was hit and set on fire. The Hurricane blew up in the air, blasting him free from the burning cockpit. It was a very long time before Tom Gleave was fit enough to sit once more in the driving seat of a Hurricane. Earlier in the day his friend Squadron Leader Starr had been shot down and killed.

By now a rapid build-up of Messerschmitt Bf.109 strength was much in evidence, presenting the greatest danger to the defending aircraft. As many as fifty were sent as escort for a force of only eight bombers when they attempted a raid on Kenley on 1st September. The bombing was so erratic that more damage was done to property in Buxton Lane than to the aerodrome.

Two days later, a shattered No 616 Squadron made way for thirteen Spitfires of No 66 Squadron arriving from Coltishall. This was also a day of note for the staff of the Operations Room. One obvious conclusion drawn at the time of the raid on 18th August was the extreme vulnerability of the Sector Operations building. Luckily on that occasion it had survived but its safety and that of its equipment and personnel in the event of a further determined attack gave cause for concern. Sited only a few yards from the perimeter track, it occupied a very exposed position. The fighter control nerve centre had to be moved, and moved quickly.

Spice and Wallis had been running a successful butcher's shop and abattoir at 11 Godstone Road, down in the valley at Caterham, for a

*Because of his night fighting success, Flight Lieutenant Sanders stayed behind to operate at night.

number of years. They closed down just before the outbreak of war and the building and the yard at the rear became vacant. Later, while searching the district for unoccupied premises, the R.A.F. discovered it and were using it for training staff in Operations Room duties and procedures. It was to these premises, in the main Caterham shopping thoroughfare, that G.P.O. engineers transferred from the aerodrome the complicated telephone systems of fighter control. Shoppers going about their daily business had no inkling of the vital work going on behind the

The shop at 11 Godstone Road, Caterham, which was used as an emergency Operations Centre from 3rd September to 1st November, 1940, and from which the Kenley Sector's fighters were controlled during the Battle of Britain. This photograph was taken after the shop had been acquired by E. Reeves in 1947. *Surrey County Libraries*

closed door of the old shop, inches from where they stood. To them it remained Spice and Wallis's old butcher's shop; to R.A.F. personnel, it became officially known as Camp 'B'.

The building remained much the same as it always had been. Outwardly, save for a thick coating of whitewash on the windows, it appeared perfectly normal. There were no internal alterations to any of the three floors, there being no time to make changes; even the stone slabs and meat hooks remained in situ. The layout of equipment was so arranged that it fitted the building's peculiarities as well as possible. The

Godstone Road, Caterham, as it is in 1985. The modern brick shop in the centre of the picture bearing the name "Cordon Bleu" occupies the site of the shop which became Kenley's Operations Centre.   *Author*

shop itself was used as a rest room and a place where meals could be taken, use of the front door being denied by blocking it off. What was once the shop's cash desk became the P.B.X. telephone exchange and Signals and Wireless Ops were somehow fitted into the slaughterhouse and cold store in the yard at the back. A small room at the rear was given over to the officers as a restroom, and the kitchen was used by everyone for making tea, etc. On the floor above, the Operations Room was over the shop, overlooking the road, with "pip squeak" direction finding tables in a room at the back. Two rooms were fitted out at the top of the building on the second floor as sleeping quarters, one each for men and women. On quiet nights, when people could be spared, they were allowed to go to bed and catch up on their sleep.

By a strange quirk of the architect's pen, right at the very top of the building was the sole toilet, totally inadequate for a staff of thirty or more people. But it coped, and its use, instead of being a source of irritation, became the object of quiet fun. Those wishing to avail themselves of the facility would often find others patiently waiting in a stepped-up queue on the topmost stairs. Normal Service protocol and deference to rank continued to be observed, and this often created an air of comedy, for when an officer laboured past the occupied stairs everyone in turn sprang bolt upright to attention.

Changes of the duty watch were well organised. The relief staff assembled at the aerodrome, were transported by coach down into Caterham and deposited at the gates at the rear of the yard. Those retiring then boarded the coach for the return journey. No one was allowed to wander about and so create unwelcome interest in the shop.

Early on there was only one direct telephone link to the aerodrome, running to a small pill box near the old Operations building from which instructions were relayed over the loudspeakers to the pilots waiting by their aircraft at dispersal around the aerodrome.

During the short period that the emergency Operations Room was in use its supreme importance in controlling the Sector's aircraft was indicated by the interest shown by some very important visitors. Lord Beaverbrook, who was then Minister for Munitions, came and watched. Prime Minister Winston Churchill also unobtrusively slipped in through the back door on one occasion to observe the progress of the battle at first hand.

Turning the shop into a usable control centre was akin to fitting a quart into a pint pot, and it says much for the adaptability of the staff that they continued to go about their business in a cheerfully resolute manner; minor inconveniences were accepted and glossed over by an intense sense of purpose which was the foundation of everything said or done. For example, the very centre of attention, the large scale map on the Ops Room table, was so badly torn and tattered that positioning of plots showing the location of aircraft was very difficult. Using their manipulating "wands" with ever greater dexterity, W.A.A.F.s persevered until pushing and manoeuvring the plots over the poor surface became second nature. No one complained, they simply got on with the job. This was the attitude shown by everyone involved with the running of the Station.

Out at dispersal on the aerodrome, life at times became very hectic. A call to "scramble" was either broadcast over the loudspeakers where the pilots sitting strapped in their cockpits on "standby" could hear it, or was telephoned to the respective squadron hut at dispersal. If the latter method was used, the "erk" on telephone duty gave the instructions to the pilots and dashed to the hut door where he vigorously rang a hand bell. Flight mechanics sitting waiting in the aircraft, on hearing this, immediately pressed the starter button and to the whirring sound of starter motors, the big three-blade propellers jerked slowly round until the engines fired, belching black smoke from the exhaust stubs. By the time the pilots reached the aircraft, the mechanics were out of the cockpits and standing on the wings ready to assist their pilots with strapping on their safety harnesses. This done, they hastily removed themselves, and on a signal from the pilot removed the chocks from the wheels. A small burst of extra power and the aircraft moved forward. Usually they taxied down to the end of the runway and took off in sections of three aircraft; on occasions, however, the word "scramble" adequately describes the situation as aircraft appeared to be going off in all directions in the race to get airborne and gain height. The quiet peaceful scene of a few moments ago was dramatically transformed by the steady throb of sometimes as many as a dozen or more powerful Merlin engines, telling everyone in the district that the Kenley fighters were off, something was "up." While climbing, the sections joined up as quickly as possible and the squadron was on its way.

When the aircraft had gone, groundcrew busied themselves preparing for their return. If an attack alarm was on, everyone was expected to go into an air raid shelter, and an airman could have been put on a charge for not doing so, but most elected to stay outside to see what was "cooking."

Life had settled into a pattern. Aircraft continually taking off and returning to be immediately refuelled, re-armed and checked, to wait for the next call to action. Each aircraft had its own groundcrew; a flight mechanic, a rigger and an armourer, who was assisted by a team of three others when in action. The final act of the re-arming procedure was to dope a small square of fabric over each gunport to prevent the guns freezing in the ice-cold air many thousands of feet above the ground, but as "scrambles" became more frequent such niceties were dispensed with in favour of patches of ordinary sticking plaster. As their aircraft was landing, the groundcrew peered at the leading edge of the wing to see if the tape had been blown away, a sure indication that the guns had been fired and re-arming was necessary. By the time the aircraft had taxied in, they knew what was expected and were ready.

As the battle wore on, even the most casual observers could not have failed to notice the steady deterioration in the outward appearance of the aircraft. The once scrupulously clean wings were now permanently streaked with black cordite deposits from continual use of the guns; smart paint jobs became a thing of the past as riggers patched and repaired in quick time.

When a machine was at "readiness," waiting for a call to take off, little or no maintenance could be done. When at "30 minutes" only work which could be squeezed into that period of time was attempted. It was only after the squadron was released, usually at the end of the day, that major servicing was done. Any battle damage requiring repair work was

The Station Commander, Group Captain T. B. Prickman, seated fifth from left, and fellow officers at Kenley in 1940.

carried out in the remaining hangar, or accomplished out in the open at dispersal. By taking advantage of the light summer evenings, ground-crews worked until the jobs were finished so that the aircraft were ready for an air test early the next day. If excessive battle damage occurred, the aircraft was replaced and, if flyable, was flown out to a maintenance unit.

Although No 253 Squadron successfully redressed the balance of No 66 Squadron's losses of their first day, by the end of the second No 66 Squadron had lost ten Spitfires.* This in itself, although very upsetting, was not disastrous, as replacement aircraft were readily available. More important was the loss of pilots; two were killed, two seriously wounded and several others suffered various minor injuries. The price of being "thrown in at the deep end," so to speak, had been paid.

For everyone, inexperienced or veteran, the air over Southern England was a very dangerous place. Large formations of Messerschmitt Bf.109s continued to provide escort to the Junkers, Dorniers and Heinkels as they carried their lethal loads to the targets. Perhaps more dangerous, similar numbers flew in fighter sweeps, roaming the sky looking for British aircraft. Anyone meeting them was more often than not tactically, and almost certainly numerically, at a disadvantage. Encounters with such groups were usually costly and right in keeping

*Five later recovered and repaired.

with the German policy of destroying Fighter Command in the air. Even full squadron strength was not enough to provide a reasonable chance of survival if you were caught by them.

After six days, the remnants of No 66 Squadron changed places at Gravesend with No 501, a Hurricane squadron, and while there an influx of new pilots brought them back to strength. Soon afterwards, one or two pilots were used in an experiment designed by Fighter Command leaders to improve their knowledge of approaching raids. The idea was to use Spitfires in a fighter reconnaissance role; when a raid was beginning to build up, they were ordered off on patrol and, by a direct radio link with Group Headquarters, information was sent back telling the composition of the formation, etc., as the raid came in. Having achieved some success with this, a small fighter reconnaissance unit, known as No 421 Spotting Flight, was attached to the squadron in early October.

No 66 Squadron's replacements at Kenley were another of the battle-hardened squadrons which had earlier fought in France and, despite having had a tough time at Gravesend during the previous six weeks, remained a cohesive and very potent force. They took over the dispersal on the northern side of the aerodrome and Squadron Leader Hogan had part of the old Married Quarters on the ground floor of "Flintfield House" as squadron offices. Their arrival caused a few problems with accommodation and several rooms in a local hotel were put at the pilots' disposal. When things were eventually sorted out, the airmen lived in four requisitioned houses down Whyteleafe Hill and flying personnel and senior N.C.O.s, for the most part, lived on the aerodrome. With the pilots of the other Sector Squadron, they were quite a cosmopolitan bunch, including Poles, Czechs, Belgians, South Africans, Irish, Scots and men from all parts of England.

Air Vice-Marshal H. A. V. Hogan, C.B., D.F.C., wrote about the memorable features of some of his men:

> Flying Officer Dafforn was one of the tallest men who flew in the Battle of Britain and was, in fact, really too big to fit comfortably into a Hurricane, with the result that his head stuck well out. Steve Woltanski never spoke a word, but was always there when there was something doing. "Ginger" Lacey invariably shot literally and metaphorically everything down with an air of complete aplomb, and his prowess was greatly admired by everyone.

"Ginger" Lacey's achievements were already well known, and by the end of the Battle of Britain he had become one of the highest-scoring British pilots. One of his most notable accomplishments occurred on the day of his arrival at Kenley. After receiving a report that a lone raider was somewhere aloft over London, he took off in poor visibility and low cloud, knowing that the prospect of finding his way back and landing safely in such conditions was very poor; in fact he knew that he would almost certainly have to bale out. After searching for a long time, and with a lot of help from the controller, he finally found his prey, a Heinkel He.111, and chased it in and out of the clouds. Both aircraft opened fire from point blank range. Lacey's Hurricane was badly hit and caught fire, but he did not bale out until he had used up all his ammunition; both engines of the Heinkel were on fire and it was on its way down. Lacey came down by parachute near Leeds Castle in Kent. Both trouser legs were burned and he had superficial burns to his face. He later learned that the Heinkel had bombed Buckingham Palace.

When the weather was fine the watchers on the ground, looking high into the sky, witnessed the struggle going on there, often several miles above them. Fighter clashes were sometimes so high that the aircraft looked like tiny silver fish as the sun reflected off them. White contrails clearly marked the pattern of the conflict against a background of clear blue sky, and remained for several minutes before being dispersed by the winds. Sounds of powerful engines and chattering machine-guns punctuated by short bursts of cannon fire drifted down to the people below. Hopefully it was the enemy seen falling, but often it was "one of ours."

On 30th August the watching knot of people out at dispersal had seen a Hurricane falling over Woldingham; their relief at seeing the parachute blossoming into shape turned to sickened fury as an unscrupulous Messerschmitt Bf.109 pilot was seen to turn his aircraft and shoot the British pilot. The dead man is thought to have been Pilot Officer Jenkins of No 253 Squadron. Coincidentally, another No 253 Squadron pilot, Sergeant J. H. Dickinson, is thought to have suffered a similar fate later in the day.

Two days later another Hurricane spiralled down; it crashed into a cornfield between Welcomes Road and Hermitage Road, setting it on fire. The pilot's body, almost certainly that of Flying Officer P. P. Woods-Scawen (one of Peter Townsend's No 85 Squadron colleagues from Croydon), was found in the garden of "The Ivies" in Kenley Lane five days later, wrapped in a parachute which had failed to open properly.

On the morning of 6th September, after being attacked by British fighters, a Messerschmitt Me.110* plummetted into the ground on Coulsdon Court Golf Course, killing the pilot, Unteroffizier Kiehn. His colleague baled out safely.

During a teatime engagement on 9th September, two Hurricanes of No 310 (Czech) Squadron, based at Duxford in 12 Group, were involved

*The remains of this aircraft were dug up by members of the London Air Museum in May 1976.

in a mid-air collision over Purley. The squadron, having been caught by a bunch of Messerschmitt Bf.109s and Me.110s, was splitting up when the incident occurred. By chance, in the melee, a Messerschmitt Me.110 flew directly beneath the stricken aircraft and one of the falling British machines smashed into it.

Fireman W. J. Carey, standing in the yard outside Purley fire station, watched the three shattered fighters falling, the German diving towards the ground at great speed, with a Hurricane fluttering down close by on each side of it. One crashed in Purley Way, near Croydon aerodrome, and the other was last seen falling in the direction of Coulsdon and Hooley. Soon afterwards, the Purley brigade was sent to where the crashed Messerschmitt Me.110 was burning in the back garden of "Kennicott", a private house in Woodcote Park Avenue, Purley. Its pilot had died in the aircraft. Before crashing, Flying Officer G. L. Sinclair's Hurricane was descending upside down in a furious spiral, the pressure throwing him against the cockpit canopy and making it awkward for him

"Grove House" in Salmons Lane, on the south-east fringe of the aerodrome, which was used as W.A.A.F. quarters during the Second World War.   *Author*

to slide it back so that he could jump out. Having overcome the difficulties, he parachuted down into some woods near Coulsdon, spraining an ankle. Flying Officer J. E. Boulton fell with his aircraft and was killed.

About the same time, from four miles above Kenley came the sounds of battle as a bunch of twelve or more aircraft were engrossed in the now familiar struggle which often decided the difference between life and death for the participants. A Hurricane flown by Sergeant R. Lonsdale of No 242 Squadron was seen to break away and dive earthwards, pieces breaking off its damaged tail section as the rapidly increasing forces of the descent took their toll. The cockpit canopy was seen to detach and the pilot bale out. A German fighter turned to shoot at the descending parachutist but was seen off by a protecting British fighter. The Hurricane dived into the ground in the back garden of a house bordering Ninehams Road, Kenley, only a few yards from the aerodrome, burying itself deep in the earth and shattering the water main in the road near the junction with Foxon Lane.* Coulsdon Court Golf Course claimed another victim, this time a Messerschmitt Bf.109 which crashed into the trees beside the fairway; it was some time before the dead pilot's body was extricated from the wreckage.

A welcome success at night had been celebrated on 27th August, when Sergeant Longman of the 148th Light Anti-Aircraft Battery, having received a large measure of help from the searchlights, shot down a Heinkel 111 with a three-inch gun. The fiercely burning aircraft hit the ground and ploughed its way across Queens Park, Caterham, finally coming to rest after partially destroying a bungalow in Manor Avenue. One of the crew, who had baled out over Kenley, found his way into Grove House, which was then in use as W.A.A.F.s' quarters. Noticing the R.A.F. coats hanging in the entrance hall, he made a hasty exit into the garden. When challenged, he repeatedly asked for the police, which appeared to be his only word of English. Another crew member when captured was found to have a broken leg and Dr Lewis was called to give assistance. The 17-year-old crewman was gripped in a state of complete terror; apparently his superiors had told him he would be tortured if captured.

Incidents such as these became a part of everyday life in south-east England. Reactions were strictly partisan: if the victim was German, it was something to rejoice in; if he was R.A.F., there was anger tempered by sadness.

Bringing in No 501 Squadron to replace No 66 Squadron's Spitfires heralded a change in Fighter Command's tactics. During the second week

*See Appendix six.

The pilots of No 501 Squadron in a remarkably serene formal pose during the Battle of Britain. Squadron Leader Hogan, standing seventh from left, when later asked for outstanding exploits performed by individual pilots wrote that "one could probably say something about every member of the squadron." *Surrey County Libraries*

in September, German strategy altered and raids began penetrating further inland, giving 11 Group Commander Keith Park greater warning and more time to prepare his defences. He took advantage of this by tactically deploying his squadrons in pairs (occasionally in threes), flying together as a wing. Where before Spitfire and Hurricane squadrons had shared the same base but generally operated independently, it became expedient that all the aircraft in a wing should be of the same type and, with No 501 Squadron's arrival, Hurricanes became the dominant breed in the Sector.

The middle of the month saw the climax of the daylight raids; afterwards the sky during the day continued to be fiercely contested, but the German impetus became more widely spread as they endeavoured to sustain an around-the-clock bombing offensive on towns and cities, primarily against London. Raids were still directed elsewhere against various targets, mostly of military importance, and Kenley was once more singled out during the evening of the seventeenth when nine aircraft were put out of action.

Group Captain R. M. B. Duke-Woolley, D.S.O., D.F.C., then a flight lieutenant, joined No 253 Squadron and later became a flight commander during the Battle of Britain. When he arrived his experience of Hurricanes was not great as he had only recently converted from being a successful pilot of twin-engined Blenheims. Granting his request to convert to single-seater fighters could not have presented a very difficult decision for his superiors to make, because by this time the R.A.F. was very short of pilots for the type. He writes about what life was like then:

The squadron was commanded by "Gerry" Edge, and Kenley and Croydon worked closely together as a wing, 253 and 501 at Kenley and 605 at Croydon. "Gerry" had been a flight commander in 605—he was an auxiliary—and was undoubtedly one of the unrecognized fighter wizards of the war. He pioneered the head-on attack and early in September, 1940, took over 253 after it had suffered heavy losses during its first week. In one sortie of ten aircraft on September 15th, we knocked out seventeen out of one bunch of twenty-eight Dornier 17's on the first attack: when I say seventeen, they were not all destroyed, but left the formation in various stages of disrepair, some being destroyed and the others winding up who knows where: we didn't stop to look: they were closely escorted by one-hundred-and-fifty-odd fighters. We suffered, I remember, one bullet-hole in one aircraft in return.

Someone who really impressed me was the "mighty atom"—Flight Lieutenant McKellar, D.S.O., D.F.C. (his picture used to be in the Mess at Kenley). He was in 605 and had two unusual feats to his credit. He shot down four Me.109's in one sortie in the morning of a day early in October, I think, and got a fifth the same day in the afternoon; he never had a mark on his aeroplane. He was shot down once only, the time he was killed. On that occasion he got a 109 down Dover way soon after dawn. The German formation was on the way home, and Mac nibbled off the last man. He then relaxed, turned his back on the sun, and was smartly shot down by the next-but-last German, who turned round with him. This always struck me as the classic example of the real expert doing the silly thing through a moment's complete mental aberration, and of the price one can pay for it in war.

Then there were amusing incidents concerning two chaps in 253—Robert Watts, the other flight commander, and a young Pilot Officer Graves, a cousin of the novelist. Watts was shot down in November, 1940, and came dangling down under a parachute. He touched down near the suburbs of London, and was soon surrounded by an admiring crowd of hero-worshippers. Bob was making the most of the situation, using his hands making the traditional fighter pilot swooping gestures, and doubtless supplying suitable noises off. At the climax of the series, as all were gazing raptly at the intrepid bird-man, a small aggressive woman burst through the front rank. From about two feet nearer Mother Earth than Bob's—who is a six-footer—a penetrating and authoritative voice said "Master Robert! Come with me. I always knew you'd get yourself in trouble." It was, as you may have guessed, his old nanny!

Bob went—quietly.

Young Graves arrived in late September. At that time I was acting C.O. as Gerry had been shot down and severely burnt. The Germans were occasionally shooting chaps down in their parachutes at that time, and so I told Graves that if he was unlucky he must do a delayed drop. About three days later we got firmly sat upon by a large force of fighters, and in the melée Graves *was* shot down, and baled out at 17,000 feet. He told me later that he was about to pull the rip-cord when he recalled my briefing and paused. He watched his boots sweep round the sky, then the cloud below, and then the sky again. He fell into cloud at about 7,000 feet, and out into the clear again at about 5,000 feet. Still he waited, revolving slowly, until, as he said, "I could see the branches on the trees". His 'chute opened—the height was given me by the Observer Corps post who welcomed him—at one hundred and fifty feet. "Delayed drop" is just the right expression.*

Another unusual feat I recall was (again) Archie McKellar who attacked three Heinkel 111s trying to do a medium-level. He made one head-on attack at about 8,000 feet and touched off the bomb-load, which in the Heinkel was stored vertically and for some odd reason nose up. The explosion not only destroyed the leader but blew the inside wings off the other two—giving a handsome return of three bombers destroyed for a two-second burst. This always struck me as a fair enough example of economy of effort and money.

253 also figured indirectly in a famous argument. The story also concerns 605, because by the nature of things we worked very closely together. Archie McKellar, "Bunny" Currant, Gerry and myself were discussing tactics over a beer one evening and we agreed that the usual fighter formation was no good. At that time, all squadrons flew around as four tight Vics of three aircraft in each Vic: once well airborne, the formation peeled off one "weaver" who flew a zig-zag course across the tail-end of the rest. We felt that this formation gave no chance of surprising the Germans because one could see the solid blob of the formation a long way away, and also it was unmistakably English. We therefore designed, and practised when we could, a "fluid-pairs" formation on the lines of the Germans' own. Using this formation we found that we could get very much higher with one or two squadrons than the Hurricane I normally operated. In fact, 30,000 feet was well on the cards, and we became rather good at operating from that height instead of the more usual 20,000-foot mark (for Hurricanes).

At about this time—late September, 1940—a certain argument was in progress about the method of reinforcing 11 Group from 12 Group. Leigh-Mallory, then A.O.C.** 12 Group, was in favour of large formations—five and six squadrons. Keith Park, then A.O.C. 11 Group, favoured the small mobile formation. Both were looking constantly for ammunition to support their arguments.

Very often in those days, liaison between the Groups was not watertight, and one occasionally never knew before take-off that the 12 Group "Balbo"† would be in the area. The incident I remember was in latish September, when I was leading 253 on a standing patrol over Canterbury. Normally, these patrols were at 15,000 feet, but I seized the opportunity for practice, and was at 28,000 in our new formation. German aircraft were reported to be approaching our area, but no more precise information was given about direction, height or numbers. We accordingly increased height to 31,000, and seeing nothing to the East and South I gazed North, almost immediately seeing a black mass bearing down from the direction of London, and handsomely below us. I recognized the aircraft soon after as the 12 Group Balbo, but they looked

*29th September.

**Air Officer Commanding.

†Named after the Italian, Italo Balbo, who became well known for leading large formations of aircraft on long-distance flights.

This Hurricane of No 615 Squadron carries the crest of Croydon, indicating that it was presented by the local town. The photograph was probably taken during the winter of 1940–41. *Imperial War Museum*

so determined that I felt they must be after some specific raid; I therefore felt they might lead us to something interesting, and turned in behind them as a sort of voluntary top cover. Feeling friendly disposed myself towards them, I never thought they would mistake me for a German formation, but I forgot to realise that our formation was still unpublished, that Hurricanes just *did not* operate at 30-grand, and that the "109" *did* look rather like a Hurricane. The Balbo, of course, did mistake us and thought they were about to be "bounced"—so they orbited. I thought they were orbiting to intercept the raid that we were after, and orbited too. When the Balbo straightened out to climb to "engage" me, I naturally followed suit. They, equally naturally, had no intention of climbing up on a straight course to be "bounced." Thus, for some minutes, there was complete stalemate, until they started to get short of fuel and retired in good order to the North, while we returned towards the coast.

About a fortnight later, I read a letter from 11 Group analysing in caustic terms the operation of the "Balbo." I remember that about eight of its trips were mentioned, the main point stressed being the comparatively short effective time on patrol. With some horror I saw one trip described under "Remarks" in roughly these words: "Six squadrons attempted to patrol for fifteen minutes in Canterbury area, but mistook an 11 Group squadron already on patrol for German aircraft and returned in disorder to their bases." The story got around the Station and was received with huge delight by ground crew as well as aircrew. I remember feeling myself that my innocuous patrol report could link me with the 11 Group report, and that if any fur was flying I was possibly going to be in the middle somewhere: the role of "evidence" in a head-on collision between two A.O.C.s seemed to me rather like the then well-known advertisement for Cadbury's chocolate entitled "Talking of Sandwiches" and depicting two burly giants simultaneously barging a weedy individual from opposite directions.

One last personal line-shoot might be of interest as it concerns those magnificent chaps, the Observer Corps. I took off one day in October with a Pilot Officer Murch as

101

No 2 to look for single bombers coming in and using cloud cover. Cloud conditions were 8/8 at 500 feet in layers, with clear patches in between: each layer of cloud being about 3,000 feet thick, and each clear band about 500–700 feet high. Climbing south from Kenley I saw, as we passed through a clear band on the climb, an aircraft about fifteen miles west of us heading north—alone, unidentifiable, but probably German. With Murch in formation I turned north-west, climbed into the next cloud stratum above, and prepared to do a sort of D.R.* interception. Kenley controller verified that an aircraft was being reported in the area I had given on R/T, and also had a track of my section: the interesting thing being that both the German and us were being plotted only by the Observer Corps *and on sound-plotting*. With small alterations of course, I stayed in cloud for about fifteen minutes until the controller told me I was within about half a mile of the "Bogey." Diving gently down, Murch and I broke cloud dead behind and a mile from a Dornier 17, and before he could hide himself away, we had clobbered him.** Although there must have been other cases, I never heard of another example of an interception done by Observer Corps sound-plotting alone, and the observers gave us for our combat report our route, time and place of combat, and location of crash (owing to low cloud, we could not follow the aircraft down through the lowest layer of cloud).

No 253 had, on average, seventeen pilots on strength, and we always tried to have only thirteen on the Station. Thus four were nearly always away at a time on twenty-four or forty-eight-hour pass. C.O. and flight commanders took time off when their personal aircraft was due for periodical servicing—either a thirty-hour inspection or after being perforated by a careless German. Thus, for example, I usually got a twenty-four or thirty-six-hour stand-down every two to three weeks, during which the usual pastime was to sleep for eighteen hours to freshen up!

We had a regular daily routine: the batman used to call me at 0445—and had strict standing instructions to call me again at 0450 and remove the bed-clothes. A quick wash and breakfast followed: I never could eat so early in the morning, but found from experience that this was the only meal before dinner one could count on getting. So one ate heartily—to outside observers—albeit unenthusiastically.

We aimed to be at dispersal by about 0530, varying of course with time of first light. Dry shavers were much in evidence at this time (either electric, or hand-operated), and there was a busy whining noise as we spruced up.

The dispersal was on the east side of the airfield, outside the peri-track south of the N.E.–S.W. runway and on the grass. 501 were dispersed around the north of the airfield. The ground crew on early morning readiness slept in the shelters at the back of the blast-pens, and hardly ever did we have less than fourteen Hurricanes serviceable for first light.

The first sirens would go about 0600, usually for a recce aircraft, and sometimes a section would be sent off. In October, nearly all sorties except for standing patrols were by sections to chase single bombers using cloud cover, but before that time arrived most sorties were by one or two squadrons. Thus, by 0630 we usually got our first "scramble"—either a squadron solo, or to make a wing with 501 or 605. With 605 we always used the same tactics, and gained height on a westerly heading, turning back over Guildford, roughly, at about 12,000 feet and thus getting our height off to the flank of any incoming raid. The ground controllers in these early

---

*Dead Reckoning.

**Operations Record Book entry for 6.10.40 states that Flight Lieutenant R. M. B. D. Duke-Woolley and Pilot Officer L. C. Murch shot down Dornier 17, making two attacks from astern. Aircraft jettisoned bombs S.E. of Tunbridge Wells and crashed in Butchers Wood near Mayfield.

days usually failed to appreciate the paramount values to us of height and background, and tried invariably to make us gain height to the south. We had learned this lesson, however, by bitter draughts of unpalatable medicine, and resolutely held to our tactics. A sample R/T conversation—until the controllers learned too—would therefore run something like this:

Self	Hello, Ground Station (I forget the call-sign), Viceroy leader airborne, over.
Ground	O.K. Vector 160°.
Self	O.K. Ground. Vectoring 260°, angels four, going up.
Ground	O.K. Viceroy, but I said Vector 160, repeat 160.
Self	Hello, G.S. your R/T not very good. Shall I stand by for "Pipsqueak" Zero? Am steady on Vector 265 angels six. Over.
Ground	Hello Viceroy. I say again Vector ONE-six-zero. Stand-by for Pipsqueak Zero.
Self	Standing-by for Pipsqueak Zero. (Carefully omitting any reference to vector).
Ground	(Would give Zero) What vector are you on?
Self	Zero received. Could not get the rest of your message. Please repeat.
Ground	I said, WHAT IS YOUR VECTOR?
Self	I think you are talking too loud. Your speech is distorted. Am 20 miles west of base at Angels 10 turning on to 120°.
Ground	Understand etc. etc. Vector 130 now.
Self	O.K. understand 130. Receiving you much better now.
	etc.
	etc.

It was a great life, and we all came gradually to understand each other's idiosyncracies.

We would be down again by about 0800, and the armourers would be on the wings with belts of .303 festooned round their necks before you stopped taxiing. They used to go at it with a magnificent will. My own crew never failed to re-arm and refuel within six or seven minutes at the outside, and the whole squadron was turned round in about fifteen minutes. We would try and get flights off for a proper breakfast in rotation, but often we were asked to stay at "Readiness" for another scramble. Of course, in the event, we sat around for probably two or two-and-a-half hours, and could easily have been released. But looking back on the critical stage the battle reached, I feel we cannot justifiably criticise the Operations staff. The tea wagons did a lively trade, and we lined ourselves with dough and chocolate instead.

Our second "scramble" would be usually at about 1130, and the same drill would follow as before. Apart from the fact that the actual targets changed, each sortie was much like the last. I did not see very much really of the big daylight raids by bombers, because they finished in September, and the fighter-bombers replaced them. But I do remember on 15th September, 1940, going in head-on at one bunch of bombers, and seeing—spaced out behind them at about fifteen miles apart—three other blobs coming up the same track. I will say the Germans certainly tried hard, but they *did not* like that head-on business. One could see the leader carrying on straight, but the followers wavering, drawing out sideways to the flanks, and in some cases just plain leaving the formation. After the second landing we usually repaired for lunch. But I never remember finishing it. Invariably I recall heaping my plate with all the nicest bits of meat and the best-roasted potatoes on view, settling myself down—mustard, salt, first slice, load the fork, and ... off went the Tannoy, "253 Squadron to readiness". I learned the trick finally of always taking the pie, if offered, and *mashed* potatoes, and making back to dispersal with my plate and fork, eating as I walked or drove in the car.

Usually three scrambles was the day's portion, and after 1500 hours we could relax. Occasionally we did go off again, but normally by 1900 we had not been needed and were released. I have known five scrambles in the day, as there was usually a late recce aircraft sent over which often came over Kenley, and we made it a point of honour that two pilots would always wait, just in case, even if we were released. Aircraft inspections and servicing went on until about 2130 or thereabouts, by which time the night bombers were droning overhead. On moonlight nights, we occasionally did voluntary sorties to try "cats'-eye", but I personally only got extremely cold and occasionally badly frightened by London's Ack-Ack firing, probably, at somebody else! By 2200, my flight sergeant could, and did, come hurrying round to the Mess with the aircraft serviceability state for next morning, and with the other flight commander we worked out the early morning "Readiness" roster, depending on the serviceability state of each flight. We then fixed who should be called early, had one for the road, and by 2300 would be tucked between the sheets. I have to admit that on noisy nights I slept *UNDER* the bed.

The most frightening feature of the night blitz was not the few stray bombs that whistled down on Kenley from above; not by a long chalk. No, the terrifying weapon was a railway-mounted 3.7-inch A.A. gun which used to station itself just across the valley to the east of Kenley. Many's the time I gently levitated into the air with pounding heart as that horror opened up with ear-splitting cracks from across the way, throwing dirty great bricks into the air which sounded like trains going backwards through tunnels. Wakened from a half-sleep, one could not for a moment decide if it was something hissing up or coming down. In fact, I rather think that continual indetermination on this vitally interesting point was my main reason for sleeping under that bed!

The squadron dispersal point was, actually, a caravan. Into this we crowded all "readiness" pilots, the ops. clerk who logged the scramble calls and times, and two paraffin stoves. One of the Germans' early secret weapons was patently the design of that double side-door. Across the top ran a girder with the sharp edge facing inwards, and although in theory twelve men should have been able to bale out through the door at high speed, somebody inevitably caught his head on this girder and bounced back into the throng behind. The said throng, having craftily remembered this booby-trap, would be resolutely pressing ahead with heads lowered, looking rather like a disorderly scrum trying to pack down without first locking together. From the moment the trapee—to coin a word—interrupted the steady flow of bodies, almost anything might happen. Sometimes he just went out roughly horizontally; sometimes the scrum got wedged in the door, and then slowly squeezed itself under enormous pressure out and down; on these occasions, the expressions of the front row, viewed from outside, were rather funny because their feet got left behind and there were three steps to terra firma. One could see the mood change from eager enthusiasm, through hesitation, to horror and final despair. On one occasion I recall a strapping great sergeant pilot, Dredge by name, who bounced off the girder, and being swept forward again, "chinned" himself on it and let the mob hurtle through beneath. That was a neat manoeuvre which aroused my admiration.

The squadron offices were in a wooden hut north of and within a hundred yards of the Officers' Mess. Administration seemed to be done almost wholly by the adjutant on behalf of the C.O. and thence to S.H.Q. Letters on operation matters were put in a circulation file and brought up to dispersal by the Squadron

Intelligence Officer, and were either read out to the pilots by the C.O. or passed around. The first motion after returning from absence was to see the Intelligence Officer who gave you any letters to read which you had missed when away. As soon as the "strays" were accounted for, the circulation file went back to the adjutant for proper filing. The same kind of organisation—circulation file—was used for signals, letters, etc. needing the C.O.'s signature: the operating rule was that the mountain came to Mahomet and Adj. was the one that did the fetching and carrying. (Tactical conferences were held at night in a pub in Whyteleafe, whose name I cannot remember;* a private room was given us by the management, who were intensely pro-R.A.F.).

One other feature of those days sticks in the mind: that was the supply of new aircraft. I do not know the chain of command, but the effect within the flight or

Air Chief Marshal Sir Hugh Dowding, later Lord Dowding, who was Commander-in-Chief of Fighter Command at the time of the Battle of Britain.
Imperial War Museum

squadron was extraordinary. If we had an aircraft shot up, say, at 1500 hours we made no effort to repair it. We asked for a replacement, and the unserviceable machine was simultaneously notified as being fit or unfit to be flown away. The replacement would arrive by nightfall, usually about 19.30, and the guns harmonised and compass swung that night. Although the aircraft would not be on dawn readiness operationally, it would be ready for air test (with squadron lettering) by 0900. An odd fact, I recall, is that in 253 the letter "A" was extraordinarily unlucky, and seven aircraft running (in ten days) were replaced until the flight sergeant begged me to ban it. We did, and had no further replacements for nearly three months!

Air Chief Marshal Sir Hugh Dowding, head of Fighter Command, was a frequent evening visitor to the Emergency Operations Room at Caterham, and those who saw him there could not fail to notice his deep

*Probably the *Rose and Crown*, later destroyed by a "doodle-bug."

The Messerschmitt Bf.109-1 single-seater fighter, a superb aircraft whose influence in the air war was considerable. This particular mark was introduced early in 1941.

Imperial War Museum

concern at the unremitting blitz on London during the hours of darkness; a time when the Luftwaffe had almost total freedom of the sky. Sitting on the dais, shoulders hunched up in his greatcoat, he spent many hours studying the movements of the plots on the Operations Room table. Invariably his party would leave very late, picking their way back through the troubled streets to Fighter Command Headquarters at Bentley Priory, Stanmore.

Pilot Officer K. W. MacKenzie became one of Squadron Leader Hogan's pilots with No 501 Squadron at the end of September; within a few days his name had become headlines in the national press and he had been awarded the Distinguished Flying Cross. The reason for his overnight fame was one daring incident. Together with Squadron Leader Hogan, he had shot down a Messerschmitt Bf.109 into the sea off Hythe in Kent, watching it slowly sink beneath the waves. Alone, with the sky to himself, he climbed to 23,000 feet and, after hearing the position of enemy aircraft over the radio, decided to patrol the Dover/Folkestone area. Soon he spotted a formation of eight Messerschmitt Bf.109s above, heading towards the coast in his direction. As he attacked the three rearmost machines, a fourth, which was acting as rearguard, flew into his line of fire, receiving hits in its tank of Glycol coolant, which immediately began to stream out. The aircraft half rolled and dived towards the coast with MacKenzie in pursuit, closing to two hundred yards before pumping the rest of his ammunition into it. To his dismay, the German fighter flew on. By now, both aircraft were low down over the sea at a height of little more than a hundred feet and McKenzie flew around the Bf.109 and signalled to its pilot that he wished him to "ditch" in the water. Not surprisingly, the German carried on homeward, ignoring the antics of the Hurricane pilot, who could see his victim steadily getting nearer to the French coast and safety. All that was required was a few more bullets and the already faltering progress of his quarry would terminate in the sea. The frustration that built up in the R.A.F. pilot during those few seconds finally boiled over and, after a moment of thought, MacKenzie lowered the Hurricane's undercarriage, intent on ramming the other aircraft's tail, but the extra drag slowed him down and his prey moved ahead. He then manoeuvred the wing of the Hurricane into a position directly above the tailplane of the 109 and brought it down with a swipe, knocking the entire section off. The German aircraft spun into the sea and partially sank; the Hurricane flew on minus three feet of its wing tip. Almost immediately, MacKenzie was set upon by two Messerschmitt Bf.109s which attacked from above and behind. Unable to defend himself without ammunition, his only hope was to stay just above the sea and try to gain the security of the land, which he finally accomplished with his aircraft in a very sorry state. Its engine, belching oil and smoke into the cockpit, finally packed up as he came over the cliffs and the aircraft made a "wheels-up" landing in a field near Folkestone, three hundred yards from the cliff edge. The German fighters had followed him to within a mile of the coast before breaking off the attack. MacKenzie was immediately awarded the Distinguished Flying Cross. A Hurricane had once more proved its dependability.

The Battle of Britain was now reaching a conclusion, with German invasion plans shelved. The Germans' opportunity was lost, if indeed there ever had been one, and they were now consoling themselves with the idea that if towns and cities, especially London, could be devastated by bombing, civilian morale would be broken to the extent that the British Government would be forced to sue for peace on terms favourable to the Germans, strategy no doubt emanating from Reichsmarschall Goering who had an excessively high opinion of the ability of his air arm to overcome all.

The Luftwaffe pilots had fought hard with no small measure of success, but they were never able to obtain the air supremacy which was such an important part of their plans for a seaborne crossing of the English Channel. Without it, the whole operation would have been put in jeopardy; it was so delicately balanced that little interference could have been tolerated if the ill-assorted collection of ships and landing barges assembled in French ports was to have any chance of success. Protection of such a large amount of shipping would have been very difficult even under favourable circumstances, and the German Navy certainly had insufficient resources to cope alone. Some protection was to be afforded by large guns sited on the French coast and by minefields laid on each flank of the invasion force, but inevitably a heavy burden would have fallen on their air force which, as it turned out, could not subdue Fighter Command and, in so doing, allow its attention to be directed elsewhere. To contain both Bomber and Fighter Commands at this time, when they were posing a constant threat, would have left so small a force uncommitted that only limited support could be given to their colleagues at sea. The thought of what the Royal Navy would have done if allowed to come to grips with the invasion fleet and any subsequent supply lines if the invasion was successful was possibly the decisive factor in the Germans' decision to call off the invasion and shelve their plans.

Throughout the summer and early autumn of 1940, Kenley maintained and supported its two home fighter squadrons in close company with those at Croydon (plus a night fighter squadron later at Redhill), and for only one short period, lasting a few hours on 18th August, did this falter. Three hangars and several ancillary buildings were lost by enemy bombing and the aerodrome surface and runways showed signs of wear and tear, but the general effect of air raids on the station's efficiency and morale was not great.

One notable change had occurred, however; the Sector Operations Centre was now established in the comparative safety of the shop in Caterham, one and a half miles away. This move was of greatest importance; the aerodrome could have been bombed into oblivion without it having any really serious effect on the future of the Sector. Hurricanes or Spitfires could have operated effectively, as they did later, from the satellite aerodrome at Redhill and, had it become necessary, they could have moved on from there to Gatwick. Plenty of warm summer sunshine prepared the grass runways and they were ideally suitable if such a move had become prudent. It is not inconceivable that aircraft could have used emergency landing strips on farmland. Transport of fuel, ammunition and spares would have been inconvenient, but not an insurmountable obstacle. Resilience was a quality proven in the nation as a whole and nowhere was it found in greater measure than in the support of the fighter pilots by their ground crews.

Having a third, and occasionally a fourth, operational squadron based at Croydon had also proved a distinct advantage; the force being widely spread lessened the possibility of a total knock-out blow being inflicted on the fighting efficiency of the Sector. On 15th August Croydon suffered while Kenley escaped; three days later Kenley suffered while Croydon escaped with only superficial damage.

Civilian engineers working for the G.P.O. matched their Service colleagues in tenacity. Working under difficult and often hazardous conditions, they restored the damaged telephone lines to the Sector Operations Room in a few hours after the August raid, making it possible for full control in the air to be resumed the following morning. Transferring the entire communications system to the butcher's shop was accomplished in a very short time.

Of the men in the air, spearheading the entire organisation, much has been written. One of the most important factors that contributed to a pilot's chances of survival was the experience and ability of his flight and squadron commanders; their decisions in the air were of paramount importance, literally a matter of life and death.

Responsibility imposed on commanders was immense. Day after day, sometimes flying on as many as five or six operations, they held their squadron together as a cohesive, effective force while it was being steadily eroded away by the fighting, and continually patched up. Replacements were often very young and inexperienced, with the bare minimum of training, perhaps just about enough for them to keep up with the formation in the air. By the end of each day, two, three or more of his colleagues would not be appearing on the strength the following day; and, when losses from engagements fought earlier in the day seriously weakened the squadron's strength, the remainder were still brought into action. Throughout this trial men like Kayll, Hogan, MacDonell and Thompson continued to inspire their weary men into continuing the effort. To them a great measure of credit is due for the favourable outcome of the battle. They endured the personal misfortunes of the fighter pilot and rose above them to carry on as usual the next day. Their leadership was of a very high order.

The men they commanded ranged in experience from veterans of the earlier battles fought on the Continent to mere novices fresh from Flying Training School who, even if they had not yet acquired the competency to overwhelm enemy aircraft, by their presence in the air showed the Luftwaffe that Fighter Command could still summon sufficient strength in numbers to remain a potent force and pose a threat to their future plans. At Kenley and other fighter stations, a force of young men of many nationalities inflicted sufficiently high losses on the Luftwaffe during the daylight hours for them to deem it prudent to concentrate on bombing by night. Their ages in the main ranged from late teens to late twenties, a time in life when the eye is clear and the reflexes are quick. To those young men must go the honour of ensuring that whatever plans were made for an invasion of Britain were thwarted in the opening gambit.

Very small raids, like the one on the aerodrome on 17th October, continued, but heavy daylight raids became a thing of the past and the desperate battles of August and September were never repeated; Hitler was looking elsewhere, making preparations for an invasion of Russia. At night, however, the picture remained the same as the Blitz on London continued unabated. From the point of view of aircraft losses, the bombardment was being done on the cheap; very few were falling to British defences.

The day after the first heavy night raid on London on 7th September, twin-engined Blenheims and Beaufighters of No 600

A Bristol Beaufighter equipped with A.I. radar, the aerials for which can be seen on the nose and on the wing leading edges. *British Aircraft Corporation*

Squadron (Night fighters) moved to Redhill from Hornchurch. They were equipped with an embryonic form of A.I. (Air Interception) radar set which made it possible to locate aircraft in the near vicinity ahead of them. The very first sets had been introduced only ten months earlier and the latest model was proving no more reliable; operators were recording "A.I. set started to burn," "A.I. set blew up," and other such comments in their Combat Reports. The new weapon was rushed into service in desperate circumstances and was having its share of teething troubles, as also was the very new Bristol Beaufighter, which had gun stoppages due to the weapons freezing up, bullet-proof windscreens icing over, engines overheating, etc. Its stable companion, the Blenheim, was considered to be not fast enough and lacking in firepower. Flying as often as possible, the two-man teams of pilot and radar operator worked hard at developing a technique with which the radar man could advise his colleague of a course which would bring their aircraft to within shooting distance of the enemy.* In spite of their efforts, the A.O.C. Fighter Command, Hugh Dowding, was not altogether satisfied with No 600 Squadron. "The importance of getting the Beaufighters into the air at the earliest possible moment has been difficult to instil into No 600 Squadron, who have been inclined to apply peacetime standards to a serious war situation," he commented. "I hope to have no more cause for criticism in this respect." The similarly equipped No 219 Squadron took over on 12th October, but they also found the going tough. Success was rare but, on the night of 25th October, the squadron achieved its first confirmed "kill". Sergeant Hodgkinson located and attacked an enemy aircraft over Kenley; it immediately turned away to the south, losing height until finally crashing into the sea approximately five miles off the South Coast. Observers saw it burst into flames, leaving a large patch of burning petrol. This was the only confirmed victory during the squadron's short stay in the Sector.

Apart from the unreliability of the set, the biggest drawback of A.I. radar was its very short range. How to fill the gap between the coastal radar, which reported aircraft approaching from the sea equally well by day or night, and the very short range of A.I. radar (remembering that at night the Observer Corps was blind, relying almost entirely on sound), was a major problem faced by No 600 and No 219 Squadrons, and overcoming this difficulty was a great challenge to the night fighters at Redhill.

During his frequent nocturnal visits to the Operations Room in the butcher's shop, Dowding was studying the progress of a scheme which was revolutionary in night fighter control techniques, having decided

*For the story of A.I. radar, see *Bawdsey—Birth of the Beam*, by Gordon Kinsey, published by Terence Dalton, 1983.

111

that the Kenley Sector was the best place in which to conduct such an experiment.* At strategically placed searchlight sites in the Sector one of the lights on each site had been attached to a radar device known as "George" which had principally been designed for gunlaying. It had been improved so that it could read height as well as bearing, thus making it possible to plot the course of an enemy aircraft passing over the Sector. After much inspired work, Major Russell, the Army officer in charge of searchlight and gun operations in the Kenley Operations Room, was achieving good results with his new plotting system.

Soon, fourteen such radar equipped ("master") searchlights were positioned to cover the known bomber route over the Sector. The experimental interception technique began with the Controller in the Operations Room being informed of enemy aircraft activity from the long-range coastal radar; at first *he* selected a raid to concentrate on but later the selection was left to the first "master" light to make contact, upon which the operators were able to plot its course and send back a stream of readings of height and position by landline simultaneously to both Kenley Operations Room and its neighbouring searchlight site, whose "master" light was to take over the target as it passed over its area. In the Operations Room the hostile aircraft's track was being plotted on a map at thirty-second intervals at the same time as the course of a patrolling night fighter was being plotted by using the usual "pip squeak" method. Knowing the whereabouts of both aircraft, the Controller endeavoured to vector the night fighter to within range of its own A.I. radar. The long finger of the "master" light pointing at the raider (no other light was allowed to expose on any other target) would assist the night fighter pilot to find his quarry. This primitive method using radar alone to bring about an interception at night was almost certainly the first to be used anywhere, and it created much interest in high places; Prime Minister Winston Churchill, Lord Privy Seal Clement Attlee, Lord Beaverbrook and several others, including Colonel Theile of the U.S. Army, visited a site in Chaldon to see the new weapon that made night interception possible.

At the time very few people, including those actually working on the experiment in the Operations Room, realised the importance of "George;" their Army searchlight colleagues were told nothing of the night fighters' use of A.I. radar.

Later, using the same principle, a further radar development

*Sergeant Hodgkinson's success in a Beaufighter (A.I. Operator Sergeant Dye) was thought by Sir Hugh Dowding to be the first confirmed "kill" when using the scheme. It was also, perhaps, the first by an A.I. equipped Beaufighter, although the pilot's Combat Report, which was written in a rather casual manner, gives no indication of the set being used. Certainly the "George" radar plots were employed.

supplied the means whereby a small independent Ground Controlled Interception (G.C.I.) station at Wartling, near Pevensey, had control passed along from the parent Sector Operations Centre, who were using the seaward facing long-range radar (also at Pevensey), and their Controller guided the night fighter to within the scope of its own equipment. Night fighters based at West Malling patrolled over the sea in view of the long-range radar and were then passed on to Wartling when a hostile aircraft appeared. When the system was perfected, and with improvements of A.I. radar sets, it eventually mastered the night raiders.

Tangmere took over responsibility for No 219 Squadron's night fighters when they left Redhill in December. Occasionally the odd Beaufighter had operated from or diverted to Kenley, taking advantage of its concrete runways, and this was one of the reasons given for the squadron moving. It was recorded that the decision to leave Redhill in favour of Tangmere was taken because of better weather conditions there, and runways to give assistance with take-offs and landings; Redhill was an all-grass aerodrome.

By chance during the night of 12th November a lone raider found Kenley and bombed the one remaining hangar, hitting it on the corner where a new lookout and searchlight post had been finished only two days earlier. Two soldiers were killed and another wounded; three of their R.A.F. colleagues were also injured.

While the Caterham shop was in use, builders were engaged in converting a large house into a more permanent home for the Sector Operations Centre. Its location was approximately three-quarters of a mile to the west of the aerodrome, and near enough for any activity there to be observed. For this purpose, a specially constructed balcony facing the aerodrome was introduced later on. The house was "The Grange" standing at the rear of St John's Church at Old Coulsdon. It had already attained some historical importance dating back as far as the sixteenth and seventeenth centuries. Once known as Coulsdon Court, before the present golf clubhouse assumed the title, it had been used as the manor courthouse from which justice was dispensed to the local populace.

Substantial internal alterations were carried out, including the removal of a large section of the upper floor to create one very large room to accommodate the Operations Room equipment. Various offshoots of the communications system were installed in several of the remaining bedrooms. Continuing with the established alphabetical sequence, "The Grange" became officially known as Camp "C" and started a new, if somewhat unconventional, chapter in its long history. The transfer of functions from the shop commenced on 1st November and the entire move was completed in two days.

"The Grange" at Old Coulsdon which became the Operations control centre in December, 1940. *Author*

"The Oaks," a large house at Carshalton once owned by Lord Derby of horse-racing fame, was also prepared in case a further move became necessary.

Moving to Camp "C" was a welcome change for everyone after working in the cramped conditions of the butcher's shop. The Old Coulsdon district also lent itself to a feeling of spaciousness which contrasted favourably with the Caterham shopping centre. Bradmore Green and Coulsdon Court golf course close by loosened out the district, which is basically residential.

Being near the golf course made the golf clubhouse a desirable property from the R.A.F. point of view and they took it over for use as a Mess; to personnel it had an added attraction as everyone was able to use the splendid amenities, tennis courts, golf course, etc., for a minimal charge. The clubhouse became the Station's main recreational centre and naturally was the focal point of social life, providing many happy times. The dances there are still remembered as being particularly delightful.

After the coach was withdrawn to save petrol, W.A.A.F.s were allowed to make their own way from the Mess to "The Grange" when going on duty, a walk of almost three-quarters of a mile, but later it was decided that a more orderly approach should be adopted and henceforth they formed up and marched along the road. Possibly one reason for this was that a distinct rut was beginning to appear in the grass where people continually walked between the little round house in Coulsdon Road and the gates of "The Grange". A new, well-trodden path clearly defined across hitherto unblemished parkland was an undesirable feature which could easily have been picked out by German photo reconnaissance.

Most R.A.F. people lived nearby in requisitioned houses. In Coulsdon Court Road nearly every other house was taken. Others in Tollers Lane, Marlpit Lane and Bradmore Green, plus houses further afield, were pressed into service. It appears that after the aerodrome was bombed it became a policy to move personnel further away and to select billets over a much wider area. The full complement of staff working the three-shift system in the Operations Room amounted to rather more than a hundred people; finding quarters for them alone required quite a large number of houses, and they were only a part of the aerodrome's complement.

Pamela Rust, a W.A.A.F. A.C.W.2, and eighteen years old at the time, recalls what her life was like during 1940.

> We were on shift work: afternoon, morning, all night, day off—and repeat, so this gave us daytime freedom to go up to London for our entertainment (lunchtime ballet, National Gallery concerts, theatres, etc.) or to go down to Brighton for the day. We were fairly mobile—hitch-hiking was a way of life and in time we had regular "lifts" to town from the bottom of Whyteleafe Hill (one a chauffeur-driven Daimler, but mostly lorries and service transport). We also cycled a great deal—the weather was fabulous that late summer; we explored the Surrey woods, rode horses from the stables not far away, swam at the Banstead open-air pool and played tennis at the Coulsdon golf club.
>
> At that time girls did not go to pubs on their own—at any rate my friends and I didn't. Good food, well served in comfortable surroundings, was much more in our line—and I note from my diary that one could eat home-made scones round an open fire in a Caterham cafe in October, 1940. After the Operations Room moved to "The Grange" there was a nearby cafe where the proprietor would go outside to "squeeze" the hens so that he could give us an egg supper. I forget the name, but the food was splendid—and cheap.
>
> We did a lot of walking too, in that cold, crisp autumn. Among our indoor haunts, a favourite was the ice rink at Purley; as struggling beginners, we would be suddenly whirled round the ice by hefty members of the Royal Canadian Air Force who, as expert ice-hockey players, were more at home on the ice than we were (A W.A.A.F.

friend of mine received a nasty crack on the skull and was behaving very oddly in the Ops Room that night and was sent off to recover). We used to go into Croydon, have lunch at the Greyhound Hotel and then go on to the Davis Cinema. There, for an inclusive one-shilling-and-sixpence ticket, we saw a double-feature programme, had tea in the restaurant and danced.

It was often more hazardous for us to return to our quarters ("Grove House," at the gates of Kenley airfield, was my first billet; "Hillhurst" and "Greenlands" were other nearby houses "taken over" by us) past the "Vandoos" (a particularly wild collection of Canadian troops who tended to fire off their guns and grab at passing W.A.A.F.s) than it was to brave the bombs and ack-ack (it is not often remembered that falling shrapnel from our anti-aircraft batteries presented quite a risk if one was in their vicinity).

At night we would cycle to the Ops Room in convoy—the first bike had a front lamp and the last of perhaps eight cycles had a rear light. I think the Grenadier Guardsman doing sentry duty at the gates of "The Grange" would rather have faced the Germans than this convoy of W.A.A.F.s, pedalling full tilt, heads down, ignoring his command to "Halt. Who goes there?" The only reply was a jangling of bicycle bells and the poor soldier was left lying in the hedge. The business of cycling in the dark created another amusing incident—one W.A.A.F. discovered that a ball of knitting wool had fallen from her basket, the other end was attached to the needles and caught up in her handle bars. So, in the pitch dark, with the help of matches, we all got down on hands and knees and crawled back, paying in the wool hand over hand until we'd wound up the whole ball. One learned to preserve items in short supply!

This may, rightly, give the impression that we all had a great deal of fun. Indeed we did—both inside and outside the Ops Room. I remember on one dull night when the table was clear of enemy plots and the weather closed in, the controller on duty (a squadron leader temporarily off flying duty with an injured leg in plaster) sat on the Ops Room table with us and played tiddly winks with the discs used for plotting. When the pressure was on, we worked hard, and when there was bombing as well, the tension was really high. Off duty, we relaxed accordingly. Everyone (there were so few exceptions that one cannot recall them) was wonderful, full of fun and enjoyment, of purpose and concern.

A vertical photograph of the Kenley aerodrome taken in May, 1941, showing how both buildings and runways were camouflaged. Before the outbreak of war the Air Staff had fought against the provision of all-weather runways because an Army Staff officer who had devised a means of camouflaging aerodromes had said that the provision of concrete runways would spoil his scheme. Two bomb sites can be seen: **A:** marks where "Sunnycroft" had once stood, **B:** marks the site of "The Crest".

On the morning of Sunday, 1st December, a group of sixteen German aircraft was flying over the district and two of them were seen to break away from the main formation and select a target in the Old Coulsdon area. They aimed their bombs in the direction of "The Grange" and were gone. Two explosions rocked the building and St John's Church, where morning service was in progress. Glass from the shattered windows rained over the shocked congregation, now prostrate between the pews.

At "The Grange" Betty Hatton was Operations 'B' Officer, receiving and recording aircraft movements via the telephone line to the aerodrome. She writes:

> When the bombs exploded an odd effect of the blast blew the glass from the window behind me outwards, saving me from serious injury. We all dived under tables or anything that was handy; I was under the table with the phone still in my hand when I heard the chap on the other end saying to me, "There has been a raid to the west of the station." I remember screaming back, "I know, you bloody fool, they have bombed us." Several people on duty were slightly injured by glass, ceilings were down and doors were damaged.

Outside, a direct hit badly damaged some cottages at the front of the church and their contents were blasted over a wide area. Bedding could be seen grotesquely hanging in the trees nearby. Another bomb had gone over the top of "The Grange" and exploded in Canons Hill causing extensive damage; a third failed to go off.

In church, the congregation picked themselves up and brushed the glass from their clothes. The service continued.

By good fortune no-one was seriously injured. A bomb a few yards either way would have been disastrous; the church was full, the congregation swollen in number by a party of Guardsmen from Caterham Barracks on church parade, while the Operations Centre at "The Grange" also had a full complement of staff. Both buildings were straddled by the bombs and miraculously escaped with minor damage.

It is now known that German Military Intelligence on R.A.F. matters during the Second World War was not particularly good, being probably at its best during the few days prior to and after the outbreak of war. In hindsight, even with this knowledge, those people involved in operations at Old Coulsdon on that day would take a lot of convincing that the Germans had not been told the location of the new Operations Room by someone, the raid coming so soon after the move. Earlier, Kenley had been under surveillance by spies, but by the time of the raid on "The Grange" the spy Arthur Owens, mentioned earlier, had offered his services to British Intelligence, who were using his radio to send bogus information to the Germans.

CHAPTER SIX

Offensive

AT THE end of what had been a tumultuous year in the history of Europe, the pendulum in the daylight air war was on the point of swinging the other way and by the end of January, 1941, all the squadrons that had fought in the final stages of the Battle of Britain had moved on. Their successors took on a role more inclined towards the hunter than the hunted. Consolidating the hard-won air superiority achieved earlier on the home front, Fighter Command steadily built up an offensive campaign over the Continent looking for the Luftwaffe which was to a large extent conserving its strength for the coming conflict with Russia.

On the aerodrome, aircraft maintenance was carried out in the remaining hangar, the cold weather precluding any further work outside. Four small corrugated metal blister hangars were constructed on the western perimeter to give protection from the weather for some of the aircraft, and new taxiways were laid to accommodate the aircraft using these new hangars.

Heavy snowfalls in the first few days of February threatened to curtail all flying but, in typical "where there's a will there's a way" spirit, assistance was sought from the local council to keep the runways and perimeter track clear.

At night German raids continued. Whenever weather conditions permitted, Hurricanes took off on patrol. The night of 10th–11th May was bright and clear, allowing all the squadrons to participate with success. Leigh-Mallory sent congratulations to the Operations Room. "Last night's successes in your Sector reflect great credit on Operations Room staff. Congratulations. Leigh-Mallory." Such achievement by non-radar-assisted aircraft at night was very rare; No 1 Squadron's Hurricanes from Redhill claimed five, with two probables, No 264 Squadron claimed two, and the Beaufighters of No 29 Squadron, equipped with A.I. radar, based at West Malling, made claims for two.

John Peel, who became Kenley's first Wing Commander Flying, led the Kenley Wing until the end of July, by which time a regular pattern of operations had become established. It was almost a carbon copy, with a few innovations, of tactics employed by the Luftwaffe against Britain the previous year. Fighter sweeps (Rodeos) were augmented by "Circuses," small numbers of bombers being sent out with an excessively large fighter escort, principally to bring German fighters up into combat. Close escort work was intensely disliked by pilots; not being able to leave their charges made them vulnerable and also inflexible, a condition alien to the axiom of the fighter pilot who always relied on freedom of movement for success and, more important, for self-preservation. It did have one interesting effect, however; the R.A.F. pilots realised and appreciated the difficulties experienced by their German counterparts earlier during the Battle of Britain.

During bad weather pairs of aircraft were sent off over the Continent on the occasional "Rhubarb," looking for ground targets such as trains, motor transport, etc. Such low-level strafing operations in bad weather were often very hazardous and selection of target was difficult; was the lorry you were about to shoot up a German military vehicle or a Frenchman going about his day-to-day business?

"Ramrod" was another operations codename coming into prominence, indicating an escort for a short-range bombing raid against a specific target with the sole objective being to destroy it, unlike a "circus." The occasional anti-shipping strike or "Roadstead" was also carried out by the Kenley squadrons. Generally speaking, the daylight fighter operations at this time proved costly in men and machines, as the German fighter pilots showed themselves to be equal to their task.

In the Spring and early Summer several squadrons came to Kenley and stayed for several weeks, but in July the composition of the Wing stabilised on three Spitfire squadrons, No 452 Squadron (Australian), No 485 Squadron (New Zealand) and No 602 Squadron (City of Glasgow), a combination which stayed together for eight months. With Kenley able to accommodate only two of the three squadrons, they each in turn did a spell of duty at Redhill.

It was a time of change, with Redhill featuring more in Fighter Command plans than Croydon, which turned towards other things. Hurricane had given way to Spitfire and was never to be seen again at Kenley as a front-line fighter aircraft. By a natural process of evolution the Spitfire itself was changing; by August all the three squadrons were equipped with the latest Mark VB version; more powerful and harder hitting, with two 20mm Hispano cannon and four .303-inch machine-guns, it was a pronounced improvement on the earlier type used during the Battle of Britain.

Paddy Finucane came to Kenley as a flight commander with No 452 Squadron and during the latter part of his stay took over the command of No 602 Squadron from Squadron Leader "Al" Deere. During a

Flight commanders of No 452 Squadron, Royal Australian Air Force, Keith "Bluey" Truscott, D.F.C. and Bar, on the left, Paddy Finucane, D.F.C. and Bar, in the middle and Ray Thorold-Smith, D.F.C. Finucane is using a stick as a result of an accident at the Town Hall, Croydon. Not very long after this photograph was taken in the autumn of 1941 all three men were dead. *Surrey County Libraries*

nine-month period, the Irishman achieved what can only be described as a meteoric rise to fame; a recognition of his outstanding ability which was given a certain impetus by the attentions of the national Press. In the light of Fighter Command's policy of luring the Luftwaffe into the air to intercept their fighter incursions and, in so doing, compel them to hold a strong fighter force in France, it is not surprising that most of Finucane's successes were single-seater fighters; his score of enemy aircraft destroyed, and that of his colleagues, particularly fellow flight commander Australian Keith "Bluey" Truscott, rose at an impressive rate.

Keeping the general public informed of the exploits of the fighter "boys" both newspapers and radio gave much coverage to them, creating, whether they personally wished it or not, national heroes. Justifiably, the issuing of such news was warmly uplifting and of comfort to a nation which had in the recent past suffered much from the Luftwaffe, and was undergoing some of its darkest days of the war.

In 1941 the B.B.C. ran a radio series in which R.A.F. personnel were invited to make anonymous broadcasts telling in their own words of their experiences, and in the course of the year this was done on over two hundred and eighty occasions. Paddy was agreeable to making such a broadcast, and when his turn came he said:-

I've been on about fifty sweeps, and most of my victories have been gained over France. I've got my "bag" because I've been blessed with a pair of good eyes, and have learned to shoot straight. I've not been shot down—touch wood—and I've only once been badly shot up (I hope that doesn't sound Irish). And for all that I've got a lot to thank the pilots in my section. They are Australians and I've never met a more loyal or gamer crowd of chaps. They've saved my bacon many a time when I've been attacked from behind while concentrating on a Messerschmitt in front of me, and they've followed me through thick and thin. On the ground they're the cheeriest friends a fellow could have. I'm sure that Australia must be a grand country if it's anything like its pilots, and after the war I'm going to see it. No, not flying, or farming. I like a job with figures—accountancy or auditing.

Perhaps that doesn't sound much like a fighter pilot. But pilots are perfectly normal people.

Before going off on a trip I usually have a funny feeling in my tummy, but once I'm in my aircraft everything is fine. The brain is working fast, and if the enemy is met it seems to work like a clockwork motor. Accepting that, rejecting that, sizing up this, and remembering that. You don't have time to feel anything. But your nerves may be on edge—not from fear, but from excitement and the intensity of the mental effort.

I have come back from a sweep to find my shirt and tunic wet through with perspiration.

Our chaps sometimes find that they can't sleep. What happens is this. You come back from a show and find it very hard to remember what happened. Maybe you have a clear impression of three or four incidents, which stand out like illuminated lantern slides in the mind's eye. Perhaps a picture of two Me.109's belting down on your tail from out of the sun and already within firing range. Perhaps another picture of your cannon shells striking at the belly of an Me. and the aircraft spraying debris around. But for the life of you, you can't remember what you did.

Later, when you have turned in and sleep is stealing over you, some tiny link in the forgotten chain of events comes back. Instantly you are fully awake, and then the whole story of the operation pieces itself together and you lie there, sleep driven away, re-living the combat, congratulating yourself for this thing, blaming yourself for that.

The reason for this is simply that everything happens so quickly in the air that you crowd a tremendous amount of thinking, action and emotion into a very short space of time, and you suffer afterwards from mental indigestion.

The other week I was feeling a little jaded. Then my seven days' leave came round, and I went back bursting with energy. On my first flight after getting back I shot down three Me.s in one engagement, and the next day bagged two more. That shows the value of a little rest.

It's a grand life, and I know I'm lucky to be among the squadrons that are carrying out the sweeps.

The tactical side of the game is quite fascinating. You get to learn, for instance, how to fly so that all the time you have a view behind you as well as in front. The first necessity in combat is to see the other chap before he sees you, or at least before he gets the tactical advantage of you. The second is to hit him when you fire. You mightn't have a second chance.

After a dog-fight your section gets split up, and you must get together again, or tack on to others. The straggler is easy meat for a bunch of Jerries. Luckily, the chaps in my flight keep with me very well, and we owe a lot to it. On one occasion recently I saw an Me. dive on to one of my flight. As I went in after him, another Me. tailed in behind to attack me, but one of my flight went in after him. Soon half a dozen of us were flying at 400 m.p.h. in line astern, everybody, except the leader, firing at the chap in front of him.

I got my Hun just as my nearest pal got the Hun on my tail, and we were then three Spitfires in the lead. When we turned to face the other Me.s we found that several others had joined in, but as we faced them they turned and fled.

The nearest I've been to being shot down was when another pilot and I attacked a Ju.88. The bomber went down to sea level, so that we could only attack from above, in face of the fire of the Ju.'s rear guns. We put that Ju. into the sea all right, but I had to struggle home with my aircraft riddled with bullets and the undercarriage shot away.

I force-landed without the undercarriage, and was none the worse for it. But it wasn't very nice at the time.

Well, as I said just now, one day I'm planning to go to Australia—and audit books.

A Spitfire Mk V flown by Keith "Bluey" Truscott and his Australian colleagues of No 452 Squadron. This particular machine is now on permanent display at the Australian War Memorial in Canberra. *Imperial War Museum*

On the last operation he flew as flight commander with No 452 Squadron (immediately prior to the B.B.C. broadcast) they shot down seven aircraft during the morning, two falling to his own guns and two to Truscott's; three others were claimed by the squadron as 'damaged'. That evening the pilots removed themselves to the *Greyhound* public house in Croydon to relax. A nationwide campaign to collect metal for melting down for munitions was in progress and anything that could be spared was sacrificed to this end. One early victim of the scheme had been the Croydon Town Hall, which was bereft of the ornamental iron railings

King George VI decorating New Zealander "Al" Deere with the D.F.C. at Hornchurch in 1940. To the left is Sir Hugh Dowding.
Imperial War Museum

from the front of the building, leaving bare the low foundation wall. On his way back from the *Greyhound* Paddy found the temptation of the wall too great, and while he was walking along the top of it in the dark, he slipped and fell down into the area below, breaking an ankle.

On his return to operations he was promoted to command No 602 Squadron and so remained at Kenley to continue his association with his squadron colleagues and his friend "Bluey" Truscott, who had also been promoted and was leading his old squadron. Rapid promotion to the rank of wing commander moved "Paddy" to Hornchurch. While leading the Wing soon after taking up his new appointment, he was returning from a low-level sortie over France when his Spitfire was hit in its glycol tank by light A.A. fire from the ground and he was forced to ditch in the English Channel off the French coast. Still under control and with "Paddy" speaking to his circling comrades, his aircraft glided into the water. To the dismay of his fellow pilots he failed to get out. So ended the life of Brendan E. Finucane, D.S.O., D.F.C. and Two Bars at the age of twenty-two. Not shot down in aerial combat, as might have been expected, but victim of a small calibre bullet hitting a vulnerable part of his machine.

His friend "Bluey" Truscott returned home to Australia at the end of March to assist in the defence of his homeland against the threat of invasion by the Japanese. A year later almost to the day, he too was killed while flying a Kittihawk off the coast of Western Australia. Its wing touched the sea as he playfully attempted to barrel roll the aircraft around a friendly Catalina flying boat. It seems all the more tragic that one of Australia's most successful Second World War fighter pilots should lose his life as a result of an unfortunate flying accident.

New Zealander Group Captain "Al" Deere, a man with outstanding qualities of tenacity and durability, led No 602 Squadron from July, 1941, to April, 1942, when he handed over to "Paddy" Finucane. Occasionally he led the Kenley Wing, for he was being groomed to become a wing commander on a permanent basis, a role which he later performed at Biggin Hill. Of his time at Kenley he has written of outstanding incidents and his colleagues.

Victor Beamish was undoubtedly the most outstanding personality of my time at Kenley. I was there on the day he and Finlay Boyd returned from sighting the advance screen of the *Scharnhorst, Gneisenau* and *Prinz Eugen* south of Gris Nez, on their now-famous breakout from Brest and passage through the English Channel. They were not aware at the time that the destroyers and E-boats they saw were in fact escorting the battleships; it was only later that further sorties confirmed this. Victor attacked and sank an E-boat which, to use his own words, "leapt out of the water and turned turtle."

The Kenley Wing made about three Wing sorties against the ships, the first of which was as escort to the ill-fated Swordfish squadron. Unfortunately, the weather was so bad that the Wing lost contact with the Swordfish in mid-Channel and they were never contacted again. Quite a few Messerschmitts were destroyed and every pilot had a strafing picnic along the destroyers' and other escorts' decks.

Personalities who were in the Kenley Wing at the time, other than "Paddy" Finucane and "Bluey" Truscott mentioned earlier, are noted below with a brief narrative of certain outstanding incidents with which their names are linked. Ranks are those held at Kenley during the period.

Wing Commander John Peel was awarded the D.S.O. for his leadership of the Kenley Wing in 1941. He was, incidentally, reputed to have fired the first shot in the Battle of Britain.

One incident I recall was the occasion when he was forced to bale out and finished up in his dinghy about five miles off Le Touquet, where he became the target for sighting practice by the German coastal guns. He was eventually rescued by a Walrus seaplane, which was also heavily fired on, and to make matters worse it was forced to taxi a considerable distance before being able to take off because of heavy seas.

Wing Commander Norman Ryder took over from Johnny Kent as the Kenley Wing Leader and led the fighter escort to the first-ever Hurri-bomber show which was by a Manston squadron, dive-bombing a target near Dunkirk. Norman was hit by flak, forced landed and was taken prisoner-of-war.

His name is usually associated with a much earlier incident off the Yorkshire coast when, after shooting down a Junkers 88 in very bad weather, he was forced to "ditch" in the sea and became the first pilot ever to "ditch" a Spitfire. He was picked up exhausted by a fishing boat which had been the object of German attacks. It was after having gone down many fathoms that he managed to release himself from the cockpit. At the depth to which he went it was so dark that he remembered seeing the luminous dials of his instruments before he got out of the cockpit. He was awarded the D.F.C. for the incident.

Squadron Leader Bill "Hawkeye" Wells was the Commanding Officer of the first N.Z. fighter squadron operating from Kenley with the R.A.F. and later became Wing Leader. He was famous for his ability to pick up aircraft at tremendous ranges, a reputation gained during the Battle of Britain which earned him the title "Hawkeye".

Pilot Officer Bill Crawford-Compton, who later became famous as a Wing Leader in the fighter world, received his grounding as a pilot in No 485 (N.Z.) Squadron in the Kenley Wing. He shot down three German aircraft on the *Scharnhorst* show and was awarded the D.F.C.

Pilot Officer Johnny Checketts, another New Zealander in No 485 Squadron who also became a famous Wing Leader, experienced a few teething troubles at Kenley. Checketts' career was, in a way, remarkable, and a first-class example of perseverance and application to duty. His first tour of operations completed at Kenley left him with a blank sheet in enemy aircraft destroyed and a minus two on the Spitfire side. Not daunted, however, he spent his six months' rest improving his flying and shooting. As a result, on his second tour he destroyed thirteen enemy aircraft and rose from flying officer to command his old squadron (485 N.Z.) within six months.

His most outstanding success, for which he was awarded an immediate D.S.O., was as leader of a section of four Spitfires when he destroyed four Messerschmitt 109Gs, and probably another, out of a bunch of eight, the other three being destroyed by his numbers two, three and four respectively.

He was shot down over France and had a remarkable escape, after being partially blind through burns for nearly three weeks, and finally spending ten days in the hold of a French lobster boat anchored in a Brittany port. There were ten escapees in all and the hold was only large enough to allow one person to lie down at a time. In addition, water was six inches deep covering the floor. The boat eventually ran the gauntlet of German sea patrols at night and safely arrived at a Cornish port. Two of the escapees were later admitted to hospital seriously ill, probably as a direct result of the twelve days (two sailing) spent in the trawler.

I personally had one incident at Kenley which serves as a good illustration of how luck plays a tremendous part in the life of a wartime fighter pilot. During a dogfight over Lille I did a thing which I had always warned my own pilots not to do, and that was to follow the enemy down. Having committed this grave error, I found myself at ground level just on the outskirts of Lille. Remembering the old axiom "once down stay down" I set course for home remaining as low as possible. On crossing the coast,

126

I was subjected to very intense flak and followed out by heavy guns who dropped their shells in the sea ahead, directly in my path. I had been in the dispersal only a few minutes after landing when the flight-sergeant asked me to come and look at my aircraft. A piece of shrapnel about three inches long and of perfect wedge shape had gone through my nose cowling and lodged in the glycol coolant header tank. By virtue of its wedge shape it served as a perfect stopper, but slight pressure was enough to dislodge it and out poured the glycol. Without it the engine would have seized up very quickly.

At "The Grange" advances in radio communications between ground controllers and pilots in the air, using a Very High Frequency system, had improved reception considerably. Speech could be heard more distinctly and on some occasions the sound quality was exceptional. One instance was when a pilot called up asking for guidance in a crystal clear voice; expecting him to be flying somewhere in the neighbourhood, the operator asked him where he was and was surprised to learn that he was over Liverpool. Direction finding using the "Pip Squeak" method had become obsolete; no longer was it necessary to carry a special transmitter in the aircraft because direction finding stations were able to obtain an accurate "fix" by using the pilot's voice transmissions alone. This innovation, introduced at the end of 1940, was working well. Receiving aerials for the new apparatus had been installed in the back garden of a private house in Coulsdon Road, with the transmitter a little over a mile away at Windmill Farm, close to Coulsdon Common.

One failing of the old High Frequency apparatus had been its susceptibility to interference from metal objects in close proximity to the receiving aerials; Kenley's were sited at Tollers Farm. Occasionally when interference became particularly bad and could not be attributed to natural causes, atmospherics, etc., someone in the Operations Room would pop along and find the farmer serenely to-ing and fro-ing near the aerials on his tractor, ploughing his field, completely oblivious to the chaos he was creating in the fighter control system.

Several V.I.P.s visited Kenley and watched the staff at work; Prime Minister Mr Winston Churchill, Australian statesman Mr Robert Menzies and Lord Nuffield, a man regarded with some affection by R.A.F. personnel because of his generosity in providing them with a number of aids to domestic comfort such as electric irons. King George VI watched an entire operation of the Wing when it went out for a sweep. He saw their progress plotted on the Operations Room table at "The Grange" and listened to the radio communications as they pursued a course which took them over the French coast at Hardelot and out again east of Calais. When they returned from what had been a series of inconclusive engagements with a swarm of Focke-Wulf Fw.190s he met the pilots on the aerodrome; No 485 and No 602 Squadrons had the advantage of being at home, but No 457 Squadron had to be transported by bus from Redhill. "Ginger" Lacey, flying with No 602 Squadron, was introduced as "the man who had destroyed the Heinkel which had bombed Buckingham Palace during the Battle of Britain," but freely admitted that at the time he had been unaware that the German aircraft had been anywhere near the Palace. The King's unpublicised visit aroused understandable disappointment among a few locals who would have liked advance warning so that a welcome could have been arranged. The only unofficial visitor ever to break through "The Grange's" tight security was a stray tomcat which was befriended and given the name Runik, which happened to be the Kenley callsign in use at the time.

King George VI with Sir Sholto Douglas during his visit to Kenley on 29th April, 1942.

King George VI meeting pilots of the Kenley Wing on their return from a sweep on 29th April, 1942.

If local civilians were inquisitive about the nature of the work there, they seldom showed it. The sight of the R.A.F. focusing its attention on "The Grange", and the strict security precautions, must have jogged even the most apathetic of minds into the realisation that something important was going on. Generally speaking, most people were security-minded. Later in the war, an off-duty officer was waiting at a nearby bus stop as the Spitfires were forming up in the air before going out to escort a group of American bombers. In an unguarded moment while in conversation with a local shopkeeper, the officer inadvertently told him where the aircraft were off to. Thinking this somewhat irregular, the shopkeeper reported the conversation to the authorities who later took steps to Court Martial the unfortunate man.

Equally, there were occasional complaints. They came mostly from a naturist camp near Warlingham, on the other side of the valley. Perhaps not surprisingly, the complaints concerned incidents of low-flying over that rather sensitive area. Periodically a pilot would succumb to the temptation to have a look. The ability of the naturists to run for cover over there was probably better practised than most.

A painting by Lilian Buchanan, then a W.A.A.F. plotter, of the Kenley Operations Room at "The Grange" in 1943–44 which provides an accurate record of the activity there during the time of Canadian Wing operations. It was exhibited at the Royal Academy in 1944 and now hangs in Bentley Priory, the headquarters of No 11 Group.

1 Monica Everley (Watford Observer Corps)
2 Margaret Woolrich (Bromley Observer Corps)
3 Patricia Prime (Maidstone Observer Corps)
4 Joan Webber (Beachy black board plotter)
5 Cpl Peggy Jones (tidying up)
5 Joan Streimer (North R.D.F. plotter)
7 Sue Love (fading obsolete plots)
8 Penny Bastable (making up raid blocks)
9 Nan Hopcroft (South R.D.F. plotter)

10 Cpl Hollins (listening to Observer Corps plots)
11 Sgt Bourne (keeping watch)
12 Elaine McDonald (Beachy plotter)
13 Janet Hyde (Winchester plotter)
14 Cpl Marshall (keeping a wary eye)
15 Mr Briers (Bromley Observer Corps liaison)
16 Miss Lloyd (Ops B)
17 Reg Sayers (Deputy Controller)
18 Flight Lieutenant Tapsell (Controller)
19 Squadron Leader "Ducky" Dear (Controller)

20 Squadron Leader Milward (Chief Controller)
21 Wing Commander P. Wykeham Barnes (Station Commanding Officer)
22 Biddy Kinsman (Tracer)
23 Squadron Leader Howard (Signals)
24 L.A.C. Nicholson (Deputy Controller)
25 Flight Sergeant Rose
26 Stella Bromage (Ops A)
27 Valerie Nunn (Ops B runner)
28 Nancy Bowden (Ops A teller)
29 2nd Lieutenant Mays (Army)

No 11 Group headquarters at Uxbridge maintained a constant up-to-the-minute picture of the state of all squadrons at aerodromes in south-east England, and it was from there that the Group Commander marshalled his forces and deployed them to best effect. Officially only "Group" could direct aircraft to take off, and this was communicated to the relevant sector aerodrome via a direct telephone line. An Operations 'A' Clerk (usually a W.A.A.F.) sat waiting for calls and passed on the instruction to the controller. If there was little activity in the air the job would become extremely boring and the clerk, like her colleagues, would

knit or do crosswords to occupy her mind. "Kenley!" Suddenly a voice
from "Group" would startle her into awareness. "Kenley here," she
would automatically reply, preparing herself to receive the message.
"Scramble a section of such-and-such squadron," the voice would
continue.

One of the W.A.A.F.s had a particular liking for the job and could be
seen sitting next to the controller on the dais, headset on, patiently
waiting for the call to action. After having spent one of her days off in
London, she comfortably dozed on the train journey back. "Kenley!"
sang out the porter as the train came to a halt at the station. "Kenley
here," called back the W.A.A.F., struggling back from the depths of
sleep.

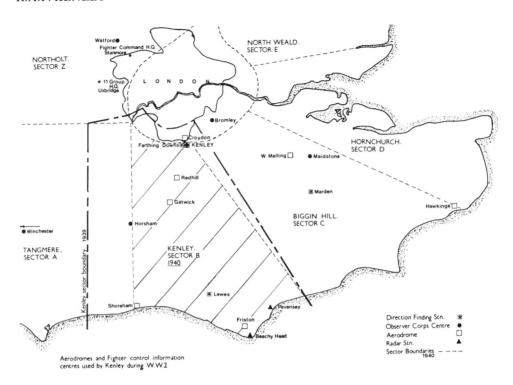

NORTHOLT.
SECTOR Z

Watford●
Fighter Command H.Q.
Stanmore
★ 11 Group
H.Q.
Uxbridge

L O N D O N

NORTH WEALD.
SECTOR E

●Bromley

□Croydon
Farthing Downs◈ KENLEY

HORNCHURCH.
SECTOR D

W. Malling□ ●Maidstone

□Redhill

▣ Marden

Hawkinge□

□Gatwick

BIGGIN HILL.
SECTOR C

●Winchester

●Horsham

TANGMERE.
SECTOR A

KENLEY.
SECTOR B
1940

Kenley sector boundary 1939

▣ Lewes

Shoreham□

▲Pevensey

Friston
□

▲Beachy Head

Direction Finding Stn.   ▣
Observer Corps Centre   ●
Aerodrome   □
Radar Stn.   ▲
Sector Boundaries – – – –
1940

Aerodromes and Fighter control information
centres used by Kenley during W.W.2

Victor Beamish enjoyed the respect and affection of R.A.F. people from the highest to the lowest ranks. Of high integrity and a caring nature, he had a profound effect on most people who came within his influence and, perhaps more than anything else, he demonstrated the quality of "leadership by example" to its very finest degree. He took over command of the Kenley Sector from Cecil Bouchier at the beginning of 1942 and continued to fly operationally when he could quite easily have elected to carry out the job from behind his desk. His age alone qualified him for a less hectic life, for thirty-nine was usually regarded as being almost elderly in fighter pilot circles. At every possible opportunity he flew with his pilots, often leading the Wing, and also coped with the demands of the day-to-day running of the Sector, which involved working long hours, often well into the night.

At this time a new German fighter, the Focke-Wulf Fw.190, began to come into service in large numbers. Whereas the Mark V Spitfire was a match for the Messerschmitt Bf.109, the appearance on the scene of this superb new fighter upset the delicate balance of the fighter conflict to an alarming degree. Vickers and Rolls-Royce urgently worked on modifications to improve the Spitfire, but it was several months before the Mark IX arrived to redress the situation. In the meantime, the allied pilots were being very hard pressed.

It was during this period, on 28th March, 1942, that a blow fell which was of such magnitude that it shook the very foundations of life at Kenley. Victor Beamish was out on a sweep over the French Coast with No 485 Squadron when he was attacked by two Focke-Wulf Fw.190s and his aircraft was badly hit. Flight Lieutenant Grant, seeing what was occurring, moved in to give assistance but it was too late; the damaged Spitfire was last seen heading out to sea emitting a trail of smoke. Victor Beamish was gone. At the aerodrome the returning fighter pilots, on learning the sickening news, mounted patrols over the English Channel

The small memorial marking Victor Beamish Avenue, which was named in 1950.
Author

until daylight failed. The following day they resumed the search, but found nothing; one of the R.A.F.'s most outstanding leaders was lost.

In the Station Record Book they wrote:

> It is doubtful whether the loss to the Service of such a leader as Group Captain F. V. Beamish can be over-estimated. No such doubt exists, however, as to the sincere regret and sense of personal loss which prevailed at Kenley when, at the close of Saturday March 29th, 1942, it was realised that hopes of effecting a rescue must be abandoned. His indomitable courage and outstanding skill as a fighter pilot combined with a great capacity for leadership and a rare sincerity which lay behind all he said and did endeared him to all those who were privileged to serve under him. Here, indeed, was a man!

There was an indication of the easing of pressure on the home front when a large requisitioned house standing at the junction of Burntwood Lane and Whyteleafe Road, Caterham, was opened as an entertainments centre. From the R.A.F. point of view it would have been a natural choice by virtue of its name, "The Turret." A principal feature of the house was a very large room which had been suitably prepared so that show business people could entertain here. On Sundays, the same room was converted into a chapel. One of the undoubted highlights, at least from the male standpoint, was when the gorgeous girls from the Windmill Theatre came to give a performance.

"Batchy" Atcherley arrived to fill the gap left by the death of Victor Beamish. He was unprepared for the current mode of operational flying, coming as he did from an earlier generation of pilots who were more accustomed to biplanes. However, the morning after his arrival he was out on a sweep flying as number two to "Hawkeye" Wells, who was now Wing Commander Flying. He has since said of the time, "In retrospect, I was clearly a potential Iron Cross to any German pilot who cared to have a crack at me." From this first flight with the Wing he learned a lot; not being too familiar with the Spitfire, he had difficulty with formation flying and keeping an eye on the leader, which caused him some concern for the safety of Wells to whom he was to give protective cover when in combat. Because of this, and the anxiety it created, he soon removed himself from such operations and in future confined his flying to a mainly individual approach.

He would occasionally climb into a Spitfire and be off somewhere over the English Channel; his first communication would be when he called up the Operations Room to ask if there was any "trade" for him. When the reply was negative he was sometimes known to comment on the "yellow so-and-so's" not coming up to fight. It so happened that one day he was out patrolling off the French coast when three of the "yellow so-and-so's" in Focke-Wulf Fw.190s latched on to him and shot him down

Group Captain "Batchy" Atcherley, Station Commander in 1942, talking to a foreign
visitor.
Imperial War Museum

into the Channel. When "Hawkeye" Wells learned of his predicament he
went out to assist and arrived just in time to photograph his Commanding Officer being picked up, in a wounded and half-drowned condition,
by a minesweeper. He was taken to Dover hospital where he was treated
for exposure and a wound to his arm caused by a cannon shell. As soon as
he was physically able, he arrived back at Kenley giving every outward
appearance of being entirely unaffected in spirit by his unpleasant
experiences. The bandage on his elbow he removed, then described the
effects of the wound on the movement of his arm, finishing with the
words "and now the prettiest W.A.A.F. in the room can bandage it up
again".

During his time as Sector Commander he set up a Station Committee
comprising representatives from all sections and squadrons and their
respective officers. This successful exercise in liaison, which encouraged

A flypast of Spitfire Mk Vs of the Kenley Wing in 1942.

everyone to discuss matters of interest for the common good, soon became a regular feature of Station life. His great enthusiasm and sense of humour earned him enormous respect from those who served under him.

Now that most of the fighting was in the air over occupied territory, being shot down meant almost certainly finishing the war in a German prisoner-of-war camp, a prospect obviously not welcomed by R.A.F. pilots. With this in mind, if ever a Spitfire was damaged, it became vital to try to nurse it back home. The last few miles over the sea were the most hazardous.

Picking up a "ditched" pilot from the water sometimes developed into a large-scale action over the sea. When he first entered the water, his colleagues took note of the position and reported it so that an amphibious

Walrus rescue aircraft could be sent out or a high-speed launch could be directed to the scene. Whenever possible, they would stay in the area and keep his rubber dinghy under surveillance until help came, whereupon they acted as escort. Noting the circling Spitfires on their doorstep, the Germans would send off two or three aircraft to see what it was that was creating so much interest, and they would invariably put themselves into an advantageous position to pounce on and shoot down the Spitfires. By carefully watching enemy aircraft movements using coastal radar, Group Headquarters could forestall this by directing the Kenley Controller to send out reinforcements which his German counterpart, using the same method, would match, until finally a big dogfight would develop involving a large number of aircraft. It soon become obvious that the right thing to do when a colleague was in the sea was to keep an eye on him as unobtrusively as possible so as not to arouse German interest.

During the latter part of the Summer of 1942 the increasing involvement of the United States Army Air Force in the European air war became evident when the 308th and 4th Fighter Squadrons each came for several days to gain practical experience with the Wing, which was then under the guidance of Brian Kingcome. The Americans had learned early on that most of their own fighters were no match for the latest German machines and they re-equipped with Mark VB Spitfires; even these, as mentioned earlier, were having big problems with the Focke-Wulf Fw.190. This substitution was made because of their requirement for a fighter which could operate as escort to their heavy bombers going out on daylight raids.

It was as part of the air cover for the Dieppe landings on 19th August, 1942, that 308th Fighter Squadron U.S.A.A.F., led by Peter Wickham (on loan from No 111 Squadron), gained some of their earliest experiences. During one of the sorties flown that day, First-Lieutenant F. A. Hill damaged, probably destroyed, a Focke-Wulf 190 during a dogfight, but one of his colleagues was shot down into the sea. Together with a 308th Squadron colleague, Captain Ramer, he flew with No 402 Squadron in borrowed Mark IX Spitfires when they provided cover for Fortresses bombing Amiens the following day. One well-remembered incident which occurred during the Americans' short stay was when a returning Spitfire spectacularly ran off the end of the runway and went careering on into the rifle range. When rescuers dashed over to the spot, they were surprised to see the wayward aircraft resting with both wings neatly folded up above it, looking as if it had clapped hands above its head.

In theory the "heavies" of the U.S. 8th Army Air Force were expected to take care of themselves and not require a fighter escort.

Flying in box formation, their combined defensive firepower was considered enough to make them safe from attack by enemy fighters. Even so, the opening phase of operations appears to have been directed at targets within the range of fighter escorts and these were supplied mainly by Fighter Command's Spitfire wings. The Spitfire's great disadvantage was its lack of range (approximately 170 miles), so activity was usually confined to targets within this limitation. Soon, U.S.A.A.F. Thunderbolts and Lightnings made possible deeper penetration into Germany, but it became painfully obvious that when these fighters turned for home at the limit of their endurance, leaving the Liberators and Fortresses to carry on alone, the bomber formations were in serious trouble. It was not until the Rolls-Royce Merlin engine had been married to the P-51 Mustang, which until that time was not considered suitable as an interceptor and had been confined to the role of army co-operation and photographic reconnaissance, that a superb fighter emerged which was capable of flying all the way with the bombers and could still meet the opposing fighters on equal terms. It undoubtedly became one of the finest fighters of the war, but it was in the earlier role of photographic reconnaissance that this aircraft first came into the Sector, when the

Squadron Leader Wickham, leader of No 111 Squadron, standing beside a Spitfire Mk V presented by the town of Sao Paulo, Brazil.   *Imperial War Museum*

Pilots of No 111 Squadron on 24th August, 1942.   *Imperial War Museum*

A Norwegian pilot of No 111 Squadron sitting in a Spitfire Mk V on 24th August, 1942.
Imperial War Museum

R.A.F.'s No 309 Squadron (Polish) operated the aircraft from Gatwick on low-level photographic runs over enemy fortifications in the Havre-Boulogne area.

From the middle of 1942 the Sector became increasingly dominated by Canadian squadrons who remained throughout the following year and during the build up to the D-Day landings in June, 1944. During this period six squadrons participated at different times, Nos 401, 402, 403, 412, 416 and 421 each playing a vital role as escort to an ever-increasing bomber offensive over Europe, and maintaining fighter incursions against the enemy.

One of the first Canadian squadrons to arrive was No 401, which was already very experienced, having served at Biggin Hill for some time. Within a month, they were enjoying the distinction of having been in the south for a year. Their squadron diarist recorded the following on 20th October, 1942:

> It was a year ago today that 401 Squadron moved into 11 Group and to celebrate the occasion a party of 32 journeyed to the Greyhound Hotel, Croydon, and a very enjoyable time was had by all. During the evening, P/O Bragg became very generous and on meeting an old friend from Calgary, presented him with two pounds. Unfortunately, the next morning he couldn't remember the friend's name.

Remembering that £2 by 1985 values would be something in the region of £45–£55, one can appreciate how generous Pilot Officer Bragg was being. No doubt the old friend was glad to remain forgotten.

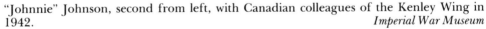

"Johnnie" Johnson, second from left, with Canadian colleagues of the Kenley Wing in 1942.   *Imperial War Museum*

The squadrons at Kenley provided the basis of what became known as the Canadian Wing. Like their predecessors, they each did a spell of duty at Redhill, adopting the same rotational system.

German raids at night were by this time comparatively rare, very little having been seen or heard of the Luftwaffe since early May, but on the night of 17th–18th January, 1943, an estimated fifty aircraft, each flying twice, took part in the heaviest attacks on the area for many weeks. The wisdom of carrying out such raids must be in doubt, because weather conditions clearly favoured the night fighter. Wing Commander C. M. Wight-Boycott, flying a Beaufighter of No 29 Squadron from West Malling, had such a highly profitable night that he was asked by the B.B.C. to make a broadcast the following day.

> Our fourth Hun of the night was a Junkers 88 which caught fire in both engines. The fire spread along the wings and back along the fuselage and it lit up the sky so clearly that we could see the black crosses on the aircraft. We watched four members of the crew bale out one after another. The aircraft went down, exploding with a brilliant flash. It was a grand night for night fighting, for the moon and cloud made conditions almost ideal.

The aircraft to which he referred crashed and broke up on Town End Recreation Ground, Caterham; it was reported that the bodies of three crew members were picked up in gardens adjacent to the recreation ground. Another of Wight-Boycott's victims fell at Westerham.

In March, 1943, "Johnnie" Johnson took command of the Canadian Wing. He arrived with some apprehension. Stories of how undisciplined the Canadians were had reached his ears. How good was the latest Spitfire, the Mark IX, which some of them had been flying since early August of the previous year? How well did it measure up to the Focke-Wulf Fw.190 in a dogfight? However, these doubts were soon dispelled. His new colleagues proved to be fine flyers and well disciplined both in the air and on the ground.

If proof were necessary, a few days prior to "Johnnie" Johnson's arrival, a No 403 Squadron pilot, Sergeant H. Morrow, while returning from his very first sweep, had run out of petrol and forced landed at Winchelsea. After coming to a stop, he called up his leader, Flight Lieutenant Magwood, and observing correct R/T procedure told him that he was all right; he then got out of the aircraft and sauntered off with his hands in his pockets. The Spitfire's wings and tail had been ripped off in the landing, which had taken him under high tension cables, over a ditch and a road, through a fence and then on through trees with trunks four inches in diameter. Perhaps the reputation for the Canadians' unruliness was a hangover from some sections of their army, who certainly achieved this distinction in and around the district.

From his very first flight in the Mark IX Spitfire, the new Wing Leader was impressed and he soon found that it favourably matched the superb Focke-Wulf fighter.

Nights were seldom quiet unless inclement weather prevented flying. German raids were few and mostly light in nature; most of the "disturbed" nights were now caused by the sound of hundreds of Allied bombers going out on and returning from raids on Germany. Luftwaffe incursions were principally retaliatory and mere pinpricks by comparison.

In the Operations Room the staff kept a constant vigil on the night sky, endeavouring to sort friend from foe. Occasionally reports came in from Observer Corps posts that an Allied bomber was seen or heard returning in a distressed condition and the staff plotted its course. Very little assistance could be given to the afflicted aircraft because its radio was tuned in to a different frequency, making it impossible to speak to the crew as they passed overhead. Sometimes a searchlight was switched on and the long finger of light moved from the vertical into the direction of a suitable aerodrome, but whether this was of any help is doubtful; the crews were usually too intent on trying to get back to their home base.

One night an aircraft was in such a bad way as it flew over the district that its pilot, feeling that it could not last much longer, ordered the crew to bale out. Switching in the automatic pilot to give himself time to get clear, he followed his crew through the escape hatch into the darkness. By chance he ended his parachute descent in a tree near the Operations Room, and was picked up and taken there. To his surprise he found the staff still busily plotting the course of his abandoned aircraft. As it carried on overland for mile after mile it created much interest, and the change in the pilot became pronounced as he gradually realised that perhaps it would have been possible to fly it back to his home aerodrome. The aircraft continued on right across the country until the plotting ceased when it must have fallen into the sea, by which time the extremely irate pilot was tearing his hair out.

By day, the Canadian Wing did a lot of hard flying, sometimes teaming up with Al Deere's Biggin Hill Wing, when as many as sixty or more Spitfires could be seen in the air preparing to go out over occupied Europe. Fighter escorts were provided for the heavy bombers of the U.S. 8th Army Air Force and medium bombers of the U.S. 9th Army Air Force, plus medium bombers of No 2 Group of R.A.F. Bomber Command. Sometimes the cover would be for the entire operation, there and back, if it was short range; on other occasions it would be provided as far as the fighters' fuel would allow or to give protection to the returning aircraft. Throughout the Spring and Summer the momentum was maintained and the pilots had little time for anything other than flying and seldom left the Station. Relaxation was gained from the usual amenities— squash, tennis, etc., which always made life on a well-established peacetime station more pleasant. On occasions, the Kimmul Club in London and the *White Hart* at Brasted provided the venue for high-spirited celebrations of promotions or decorations.

Plans were already being made for the liberation of German-held Europe, and "Johnnie" Johnson and his colleagues of the Canadian Wing moved to a newly constructed airstrip at Lashenden in Kent to condition themselves for the coming offensive. While continuing the usual pattern of operations, escorts, sweeps, and so on, their lifestyle on the ground changed dramatically. The comfortable Mess at Kenley had given way to very spartan accommodation under canvas, where the food was prepared in field kitchens and eaten using a less ornate form of tableware. When the time came, they had to be an entirely self-sufficient mobile unit capable of operating from forward airstrips. They were now transferred to No 83 Group of the recently formed 2nd Tactical Air Force, and were renamed No 127 Airfield (later 127 Wing). "Johnnie" Johnson was no longer with them on their return to Kenley just over two months later; he had been grounded for a period of rest before the big offensive.

During what the Americans termed their "Big Week" in February, 1944, when they carried out massive daylight raids against the German aircraft industry, two of their heavy bombers, a B-17 Flying Fortress and B-24 Liberator, found their way into Kenley. Damaged and with wounded crew on board, they successfully risked emergency landings on what for them were Kenley's perilously short concrete runways. One made a first unsuccessful attempt to land and had to go round again before making a successful second try. Two Thunderbolts of the fighter escort also arrived. One of the watchers who saw them leave the following day later commented, "When they started their take-off run it looked as if the tail fin of the aircraft was half way up the stairs of the Officers' Mess." Having left some heavy equipment behind, the lightened aircraft made a safe departure.

When No 421 Squadron (R.C.A.F.) left on 19th April, 1944, to join their colleagues at Tangmere prior to D-Day, few realised that for Kenley it was the end of an era.

CHAPTER SEVEN

"Doodle-bugs" and Gliders

AS THE Spitfires took off and climbed away, setting course for their new base, a new chapter in the Station's history began. The war was about to move on; no longer would the aerodrome be so important in home air defence, a fact that had already been realised the previous month when Kenley Sector was taken over by Biggin Hill.

In May, with the squadrons gone and everything quiet, remaining personnel were directed into a massive cleaning up programme.

On the night of 15th June, 1944, the "alert" roused people from the depths of sleep and sent them scurrying into air raid shelters as an odd-sounding aircraft was heard approaching London at high speed. This distinctive strident engine sound was to create fear whenever it was heard during the succeeding weeks; fear which turned to terror when the noise abruptly ceased as the engine cut out. For then everyone knew that a V.1 flying bomb filled with nearly a ton of explosive was on its way to earth; possibly on top of them, hopefully somewhere else, always with the same sickening results.

The V.1, a small pilotless aircraft, was without sophisticated guidance and once launched was beyond ground control. Usually it flew a straight course and was incapable of making evasive manoeuvres; a characteristic which British Scientific Intelligence had learned several months earlier and considered when preparing plans to combat the weapon. Anti-aircraft guns and the fastest fighter aircraft of the day each operated in their own segregated zones in the path of the bombs. As a last line of defence, barrage balloons were concentrated in large numbers on the approaches to London, the principal target.

With the squadrons in France supporting the 6th June D-Day invasion armies, Kenley, like other Fighter Command aerodromes, remained quiet. It was with some amusement that people there noticed that balloons were rapidly becoming the principal function of their near neighbour at Biggin Hill. The smiles were short lived, however; a cursory glance at the map clearly showed that if a line were drawn around the south and south-eastern approaches to London it included Kenley; it would only be a matter of time before a similar fate befell themselves. Nine days after the first V.1, or "doodle-bug" as the new weapon became known, fell in the district, it happened.

144

Squadron Leader Pickup, no doubt wiping a tear from his eye, wrote in the Station Record Book:

24th June, 1944.
At about 18.45 hours on this fatal Saturday, the first of an incredible number of these monstrosities ascended lousily into the sky in a position uncomfortably near the Officers' Mess, and by the end of Sunday, 25th June, 1944, the ambient air was bespattered with a bevy of bloated bladders which floated with bovine content and cat-like detachment in the heavens.

And on 28th June, 1944

The history of this unit for the remainder of the month consists of bladders, more bladders and still more bladders. Surely never since that long forgotten dawn which revealed for the first time the existence of the North and South Downs can so evil a blight have settled over the South East Counties.

Small air lanes were arranged in the balloon screen through which aircraft were able to navigate. In her book *Golden Wings*, Alison King describes how, using these, girls of the Air Transport Auxiliary delivered a batch of ten Tempests for use by one of the defence squadrons engaged in operations against the V.1s. One aircraft lost part of the engine cowling and cockpit floor while en route, but made a successful high-speed landing without coming to harm. Entirely unconcerned, the girl climbed out of the damaged aircraft and joined her pilot colleagues, waiting in an Anson, and within minutes they were airborne on their way back home.

Despite the dangers of flying in balloon-infested skies, pilots were known to continue the chase after their prey through the area, trying all the time to destroy the flying bomb before it reached London. One flying bomb roared over the western approach to the aerodrome at low height with a fighter in hot pursuit, shooting at it as hard as he could go. The bomb rapidly lost height and finally collided with an oak tree near Old Lodge Lane.

The "doodle-bug" crisis came to an end when the launching sites on the Continent were overrun by the advancing Allied armies, but before this happy situation occurred the defences had become so well organised and efficient that only a small percentage of those launched were getting through. Towards the end, the lion's share of the credit went to the anti-aircraft guns sited on the coast, who were achieving an incredibly high destruction rate.

During the latter part of the "doodle-bug" bombardment, a totally new German weapon began to appear, the V.2 long-range rocket, against which there was no defence. No warning engine sound this time; it simply fell out of the sky from a great height and at great speed.

In September, when the end of the European war appeared to be in sight, plans were made for disarming the Luftwaffe and Bushey Park became Disarmament Headquarters; at Kenley No 8302 Wing was formed to become the Disarmament School. Personnel were given technical training, equipped with motor transport, and formed into self-sufficient units to be ready when the time came. By December, approximately 300 officers and 1,200 men had been through the school and were equipped for mobilisation when called forward by the 2nd Tactical Air Force.

On 7th May, 1945, hostilities in Europe ceased, but units continued to be sent out until August. As the advancing armies had liberated occupied countries, the Mobile Disarmament Units had covered France, Austria, Norway, Denmark, Holland and Belgium by the end of the Summer.

Motivated by the forced stimulus of war, aviation science had made rapid strides; where in 1939 it was the biplane that still dominated the aerodrome scene, by the end of the war aircraft design had advanced so rapidly that a new aviation age was already in being, with a new power source, the jet engine. In the air its advantages in performance were obvious; on the ground, however, it was a different story. The new Meteor jet fighters, which in 1945 were replacing conventional piston-engined types, required a much longer take-off run and their higher landing speed also used a far greater length of runway, something which Kenley was unable to offer; perhaps the most important factor when it had been decided to transfer control of the Sector to Biggin Hill.

In September, 1945, a small detachment of Air Ministry (A12g) scientists arrived to arrange for the reception, storage and subsequent evaluation of captured German aircraft equipment being sent over from the Continent by the Air Disarmament Units. With the aerodrome functioning at a greatly reduced level all security and other arrangements for the unit, which had taken over the blister hangars, was left to the unit itself.

Air Transport became the prime employment during the months succeeding the war, but in 1947 a reduction in the size of the Air Transport force made way for the headquarters of No 6 (Eastern Reserve) Group to move in from Rickmansworth under the command of Sir Harry Broadhurst, K.B.E., C.B., D.S.O., D.F.C., A.F.C. The Senior Officer, Administration, Wing Commander S. Mackenzie, O.B.E., was appointed also as Station Commander; later, as Kenley's commitments increased, approval was given for the establishment of a squadron leader as station commander and the post was filled by Squadron Leader R. E. Kirkby, D.F.C.

Soon after the war, the requisitioned houses in R.A.F. possession were returned to private ownership. "The Grange," used for a long time as an Operations Centre, was restored and handed back. In Caterham Valley, the old butcher's shop in Godstone Road, from which for sixty-one days, including the height of the Battle of Britain, the Sector's aircraft were controlled, was acquired by E. Reeves in 1946 and used as a builders' merchants and general ironmongery shop. It served in this capacity until 1970, when it became vacant for several years before being demolished. A frozen food centre with local council offices on the first floor now stands on the site.

With some reluctance the Air Ministry reopened Hayes Lane for public use, effectively isolating a small slice of the aerodrome on which blast pens had been constructed and making the roadway the new western boundary. Mr Rowlins set up a small teashop there, often patronised by members of a party of German prisoners-of-war who were employed in redecorating aerodrome buildings. They were later given permission to go into Caterham and could occasionally be seen sampling the local brew there.

The main entrance to the Kenley aerodrome in Salmons Lane, with the Guardroom on the left. This photograph dates from 1974. *Author*

In 1949, a Royal Auxiliary Air Force Air Observation Post Squadron (No 661) was formed, using Tiger Moths and Austers.

Command of No 61 Group was taken over by Air Commodore (now Air Chief Marshal Retired) T. N. McEvoy, C.B., C.B.E.

A film unit used the aerodrome for outdoor scenes when making the film "Angels One Five," a fictitious story about the Battle of Britain starring Michael Denison and Dulcie Gray. Also in the cast was Cyril Raymond, playing the part of a fighter controller, a role which he knew remarkably well; during the war he performed the role in reality in the Kenley Operations Room. Another film company came and made parts of the film "Reach for the Sky," taken from Paul Brickhill's biography of Douglas Bader. This time it was Kenneth More who played the leading role; the aerodrome once more vibrated to the magical sound of the Merlin engines of Spitfires and Hurricanes.

For many years flying activity remained light and uneventful, with the occasional Anson or small aircraft unobtrusively slipping in and out. There were exceptions. A French Vautour jet, mistaking Kenley for Biggin Hill during the *Daily Mail* Air Race, landed on the short runway with unhappy consequences to the aircraft, which finished up in the bushes at the Whyteleafe end of the longer runway; it was quickly repaired and flown away. Other jets, a Meteor and a Hunter, also experienced similar fates when making emergency landings. One runway was maintained for many years for this purpose. The Station's history since the early 1960s showed a steady rundown of activity, and by the early Seventies it had become little more than a dormitory area for Ministry of Defence personnel employed elsewhere. A number of early buildings had been demolished on the southern side to make way for Married Quarters; a programme started in 1956 with further additions in 1964. These were taken over by the Army in October, 1977, and now serve families of soldiers stationed at Caterham Barracks.

After closure in March, 1974, the Officers' Mess remained derelict and was subjected to repeated attacks by vandals; despite this the building structurally remained in good shape. It was put up for sale, but remained in Ministry of Defence ownership until 1980 when the Home Office bought it for conversion into a radio technology laboratory, which was completed in late 1982, then handed over to the Board of Trade. Being in a relatively isolated position, the building was chosen because of the requirement for their work to be done in an area of low electrical interference.

Keeping an R.A.F. "presence," other than a gliding school, is now firmly in the hands of the Portcullis Club, standing to the front of the Officers' Mess, run by members of the Caterham Branch of the Royal Air

The Officers' Mess, which closed on 1st March, 1974. It is now a radio technology laboratory.   *Author*

Forces Association.* In 1976 they organised a fund-raising air show to aid victims of the I.R.A. public house bombing in Caterham. Since then, air shows have been held in 1978 and 1980 in aid of R.A.F. charities.

The aerodrome was widely featured in a book by the aviation historian Alfred Price, whose interest centred on just one day of the Battle of Britain, 18th August, 1940; his analysis concluded that this day was "the hardest day", which later became the title of the book. It was while he was carrying out his research that Alfred Price invited veteran members of 9 Staffel, Kampfgeschwader 76, the German unit most involved in the spectacular 18th August raid, to come to Kenley. The last time they had seen the aerodrome was from the cockpits of their Dorniers at treetop height. The day of their visit, 25th August, 1978, was warm and sunny, not unlike that eventful day thirty-eight years earlier. The ex-Luftwaffe aircrew met several ex-R.A.F. personnel who were on duty at the aerodrome that day: Group Captain Tom Prickman, the then Sector Commander, ex-W.A.A.F. Peggy Bray, Reg Sheldrake and Cliff Kenyon. Also present was No 111 Squadron pilot Harry Newton, who

*In December, 1980, members successfully negotiated a new seven-year lease on their club building.

was shot down. The spokesman for the German party, Guenther Unger, presented Group Captain Prickman with a large photograph showing the Dorniers of Kampfgeschwader 76 flying a few feet above the waves of the English Channel, about to make their landfall near Beachy Head while on their way to raid Kenley.

Because of the elaborate tactics employed during the attack and the use of KG 76, the specialist low-level unit, Guenther Unger was asked whether the Germans realised the importance of the Sector aerodrome to British fighter defences. "No, as far as we knew it was just another aerodrome," he replied. Kenley's secret had been kept.

After being shown around the now somewhat dilapidated aerodrome, the party was provided with a buffet tea and other refreshments by members of the Portcullis Club. Where nearly four decades earlier there had been a deep sense of hatred between German and Briton, it was noticeable that now an atmosphere of mutual respect prevailed.

Later, one member of the German party left for Hurst Green and met the owner of the house his crashing Dornier had badly damaged on that fateful day in 1940.

Soon after six o'clock on the morning of 23rd October, 1978, an emergency call was put through to the local fire station and eight appliances with fifty firemen raced to the aerodrome to fight a fire which was consuming the remaining hangar. By the time they arrived, there was no hope of saving the building and it became completely gutted. However prompt or skilful the firemen, it is difficult to imagine them being able to do anything once a fire got going; the roof was the original fabric of wood and bituminous roofing felt, with no resistance to fire. The loss of the last of the 1917 hangars was historically a severe blow, made all the more depressing by the loss of all No 615 Squadron Gliding School's aircraft and equipment which had been housed in it. Although the Air Training Corps school's activities were curtailed throughout the following year, in February, 1980, Sedbergh gliders could once more be seen feeling their way in the air above Kenley. By coincidence they are housed, at the time of writing, in a portable Bessonneaux hangar sited near the Officers' Mess. It was in hangars of basically similar design that fighting machines were assembled at Kenley when it first began in 1917; the wheel has turned full circle.

Happily the gliding school, which in 1955 took over the work of No 143 Squadron School, continues to thrive and provides local lads from Air Training Corps squadrons with the facilities to gain their Gliding

A Sikorski HH-53 Jolly Green Giant helicopter of the United States Air Force giving a display at the Kenley Airshow of 1978. *Author*

The oldest flying de Havilland Tiger Moth carrying a young lady standing on the wing at the Kenley airshow on 11th June, 1978. *Author*

Proficiency Certificates. It is now under the command of Flight Lieutenant John Coomber, who took over on the retirement in 1984 of Flight Lieutenant Alex Watson, who had served with the school for twenty-nine years. Together with Flight Lieutenant Mike Edwards, as Chief Flying Instructor, and three fellow officers, John Coomber maintains the Kenley flying tradition. On some days, depending on weather conditions, the daily tally exceeds one hundred winch launchings. Many lads with an adventurous spirit, somewhat akin to their Kenley predecessors, gain their first experience of the joys of flight at Kenley.

A clearance of buildings in the vicinity of the Officers' Mess which did not figure in the Home Office plans for the radio laboratory began in October, 1980. "Flintfield House" and the old Operations Block were demolished and a tall security fence now bounds the area.

A similar fate befell the Bellman hangar which had been erected on the site of the old No 5 Belfast hangar in the early 1950s; officially condemned as being unsafe, it was dismantled in February, 1983.

On the 12th July, 1983, fifty-two acres of land on the north-east perimeter of the aerodrome were returned for public use in a transaction with the City of London who, after a certain amount of clearing and tidying, will reopen it to the public as an extension of Kenley Common.

Happily, through the Portcullis Club, No 450 Squadron Air Training Corps, and the Gliding School, aviation and aviation interests continue on the site which saw much of the development of military aviation and which, during 1940, achieved lasting fame as one of the most important pieces of land in Great Britain.

Gliders of the Air Training Corps Gliding School on the aerodrome at Kenley in 1984. Many air-minded lads gain their first experience of flying at Kenley.   *Author*

Bibliography

Barnes, C. H. *Handley Page Aircraft since 1907.* Putnam.

Bickers, R. T. *Ginger Lacy, Fighter Pilot.* Pan Books.

Brickhill, Paul. *Reach for the Sky.* William Collins.

Bruce, J. M. *British Aeroplanes 1914–1918.* Putnam.

Cluett, Douglas; Nash, Joanna; and Learmonth, Bob. *Croydon Airport: The Great Days, 1928–1939.* London Borough of Sutton Libraries and Arts Services.

Cluett, Douglas; Bogle, Joanna; and Learmonth, Bob. *Croydon Airport and the Battle for Britain, 1939–1940.* London Borough of Sutton Libraries and Arts Services.

Donahue, Arthur Gerald. *Tally Ho! Yankee in a Spitfire.* Macmillan.

Holmes, Wing Commander A. *Air Mail,* June, 1947.

Johnson, "Johnnie". *Wing Leader.* David & Charles.

Jones, H. A. *The War in the Air.*

King, Alison. *Golden Wings.* White Lion Publishers.

Masters, David. *So Few.* Eyre & Spottiswoode.

Penrose, Harald. *British Aviation—The Great War and Armistice 1915–1919.* Putnam.

Price, Alfred. *Battle of Britain—The Hardest Day.* Macdonald & Jane's.

Pudney, John. *A Pride of Unicorns.* Old Bourne.

Ramsey, Winston (ed). *The Battle of Britain—Then and Now.* After the Battle.

Reid, J. P. M. *Some of the Few.* Macdonald.

Robertson, Bruce. *Sopwith, The Man and His Aircraft.* Harleyford Publications.

Wright, Robert. *Dowding and the Battle of Britain.* Macdonald.

Croydon Advertiser.

We Speak from the Air. H.M.S.O.

[*Crown Copyright Reserved.*

Kenley
Aircraft Acceptance Park.

BYE-LAWS

Made by His Majesty's Principal Secretary of State for the War Department under the provisions of the Military Lands Acts, 1892 to 1903, as amended by the Defence of the Realm Regulations, made under the Defence of the Realm Consolidation Act, 1914.

LONDON:

PRINTED FOR HIS MAJESTY'S STATIONERY OFFICE, BY HARRISON AND SONS, ST. MARTIN'S LANE, PRINTERS IN ORDINARY TO HIS MAJESTY

———

1917.

BYE-LAWS

Made by His Majesty's Principal Secretary of State for the War Department under the provisions of the Military Lands Acts, 1892 to 1903, as amended by the Defence of the Realm (Consolidation) Regulations, made under the Defence of the Realm Consolidation Act, 1914.

---

1. The area of land affected by these Bye-laws (hereinafter called "the Area") is situated in the Parishes of Coulsdon and Caterham in the County of Surrey, and comprises Kenley Common and adjoining lands, being more precisely described in the Schedule annexed hereto.

2. Persons desiring to pass through the area by the footpaths therein, or along the road situate on the west side of the Common from a point about 60 yards north of Coulsdon Cottages to a point about 100 yards south of Garston Hall, will, on the understanding that they do so at their own risk in all respects, be permitted to do so if in possession of a pass or permit for the purpose, or otherwise duly authorised by any Officer, Warrant Officer, Non-commissioned Officer, Military Police, or other person for the time being on duty in the area; but save as aforesaid, no person shall enter or remain within the area, and all footpaths therein are closed until further notice.

3. Notice boards with a copy of these Bye-laws will be placed where any footpath enters the area.

The following persons, namely :—

(i) The Officer in charge of the area;

(ii) Any Officer, Warrant Officer, Non-commissioned Officer or Military Police for the time being under the Command of the Officer in charge;

(iii) Any person authorised in writing under the hand of the said Officer in charge;

(iv) Any Constable,

shall have power and are hereby authorised :—

(i) To remove from the area and take into custody without warrant and bring before a Court of Summary Jurisdiction, as provided by the Military Lands Acts, 1892 to 1903, to be dealt with according to law, any person contravening Bye-law No. 2.

(ii) To remove from the area any vehicle, animal or thing found thereon.

4. Any person doing anything prohibited by or otherwise contravening Bye-law No. 2 shall be deemed to commit an offence against the same, and is, under the said Acts, liable on conviction to a fine not exceeding FIVE POUNDS.

5. Copies of these Bye-laws can be obtained at Headquarters, Kenley Aircraft Acceptance Park.

6. These Bye-laws shall come into force forthwith.

Dated this 23rd day of August One thousand nine hundred and seventeen.

(Signed)   R. H. BRADE,
On behalf of His Majesty's Principal Secretary of State for the War Department.

SCHEDULE.

The land to which the foregoing Bye-laws apply is situate between Garston Hall, Golf Road, Kenley Lane and Stumps Lane on the North, and that portion of the Coulsdon Common and Warlingham Railway Station Road, from Hillhurst House to Grove House on the South, and between Waterhouse Farm and Neville House on the West, and Whyteleaf House and Flintfield House on the East.

(B19376) Wt. w. 6677—P3027 100 8/17 H & S P.17/636.

APPENDIX TWO

Facts and Dimensions of Interest

Bessoneaux Hangars

The English standard hangar was 20 × 24 metres and weighed 9½ tons. It required five lorries to move it short distances, and six for long journeys. This was the size of hangar in use at the Aircraft Acceptance Park in 1917.

Sheds

Seven Belfast-type sheds were built in 1917–18.
Dimensions were:
Length   170 feet
Width   160 feet, which was in fact classed as two sheds. Thus each building had an 'A' and a 'B' shed, so making No 1 building, sheds 1A and 1B, No 2 building, 2A and 2B, etc.
Handley Page shed (Hayes Lane) was constructed in 1919.
Dimensions were:
Length   180 feet
Width   510 feet
Note Royal Air Force use of the word "shed" remained until the 1930s, when the word "hangar" officially superseded it (*hangar* being the French word for shed).

Runways, etc.

Two runways were laid in 1939–40, 50 yards wide and 800 yards long, and later extended, the NW–SE runway becoming 1,000 yards and the NE–SW runway, 1,200 yards.
A 50-foot perimeter track was laid in 1939–40.

Blast Pens

Constructed 1940 of 'E' shape pattern, all having two bays and with an overall width of either 150 feet or 190 feet and a depth of 80 feet to the rear section, which incorporated an air raid shelter.

The two projecting side walls were made of 12-inch thick, 9 feet high concrete centres, with earth banked up each side, thus forming a triangular shape on an 18 feet wide base. Centre dividing walls were of the same dimensions but were of brick construction instead of concrete.

It was originally planned to use narrow taxiways off the perimeter track serving up to three pens, but this idea was sensibly dropped in favour of each pen having its own wide concrete apron that joined the track directly.

158

Forward and Satellite Aerodromes

There was much confusion in official circles about what constituted a "Satellite" aerodrome as opposed to a "Forward" aerodrome. At various times Croydon and Redhill were referred to as both Forward and Satellite. During the period when Redhill was thought to be a Forward aerodrome, someone ruled that all aerodromes within a ten-mile radius of a parent Sector Station were satellites; when it was pointed out that the Forward aerodrome at Redhill was only six miles from Kenley it was suggested that the criterion should be the importance of the individual aerodrome to the Sector. As late as 1942 Fighter Command were still doggedly asking the Air Ministry for clarification.

The Diversion of Hayes Lane

At a meeting of the Urban District of Coulsdon and Purley Council on 24th July, 1939, a tender submitted by Mears Bros. (Contractors) Ltd. of £13,492. 2s. 8d. was accepted for the work. The clerk was instructed to communicate with the Air Ministry with regard to an interim payment towards the cost. The council was advised in a letter dated 21st March, 1940, from the Commanding Officer at Kenley that the new road was to be closed for the duration of the war; in fact, it was not reopened until 26th June, 1946.

The last of the 1917 hangars, originally 3A–3B, which was destroyed by fire on 23rd October, 1978. The watch tower can be seen at the right-hand side of the hangar. *Author*

Aircraft Acceptance Park and Aerodrome

Kenley, together with Aircraft Acceptance Parks No 8 Lympne, No 2 Hendon and No 10 Brooklands, came under No 1 (London) Acceptance Group.

The organisation of a 2 Section Park, such as Kenley, was made up of the following: Aeroplane Erection Sub Section, Engine Testing and Tuning Sub Section, Gun Testing, Instruments and Compass Sub Section, Test Flight and Despatch Section, Stores Account and Motor Transport Section, Transport, and Personnel.

Contemporary records show that the number of people employed at the Park remained constant (229) at least until September, 1917, but by 12th December, 1917, this had increased to 323. This figure was made up of:

Park Commander		1	Flight Sergeants	5
Equipment Officers	1	2	Sergeants	7
„　　　　„	2	4	Corporals	11
„　　　　„	3	2	1 Air Mechanics	36
Flight Commanders		2	2　„　　　„	115
Flying Officers		19	3　„　　　„	74
Warrant Officer		1	Women	44

Rates of pay for the above were (approx.)

		Per Day			*Per Year*		
		£	s.	d.	£	s.	d.
Park Commander		1	9	9½	543	14	0
Adjutant		1	3	3½	425	1	6
Equipment Officer	1	1	8	3½	516	6	6
„　　　　„	2	1	1	3½	388	11	6
„　　　　„	3		15	3½	279	1	6
Flight Commander		1	8	9½	525	9	0
Flying Officer		1	3	3½	425	1	6
Warrant Officer			10	0	182	10	0
Flight Sergeant			7	0	127	0	0
Corporal			5	0	91	5	0
1 Air Mechanic			4	0	73	0	0
2　„　　　„			2	0	36	10	
3　„　　　„			1	0	18	5	0
		Per week					
Women (Average)		1	5	0	65	8	0

The annual wage bill amounted to £26,883 14s. 0d.

In October, 1918, the Aerodrome Board recorded the following appraisal of Kenley in their Quarterly Survey. As can be seen, the number of personnel had increased to 844; this was nearly double the recommended War Establishment for a 2 Section Park.

KENLEY
No. 7 Aircraft Acceptance Park (S.E. Area; Technical Group)

LOCATION — England, Surrey, 5 miles south of Croydon (pop. 170,000) and 15 miles south of Charing Cross. Croydon Aerodrome is 4 miles to the north and Biggin Hill Aerodrome 6 miles to the west.

Railway Station — Upper Warlingham, 1 mile
Road — A second-class road passes the site.

FUNCTION — (a) Aircraft Acceptance Park (2 Sections, 1 Handley Page Section and 1 Storage Sub-section). Acceptance and Delivery Work, including erection, testing, fitting of instruments, guns, etc., and delivery by air or storage (in accordance with allotments made by the Directorate of Aircraft Equipment, to meet requirements) of the following machines received from the contractors shown:

Type of Machine	Contractor
Handley Page	Croydon Assembly
D.H.9	Cubitt & Co.
Dolphin	Darracq
Camel	Hooper (Chelsea)
R.E.8	Napier & Co.
D.H.9	Short
Dolphin	Sopwith Aviation Co.
Salamander	Sopwith Aviation Co.
S.E.5	Vickers (Crayford)
D.H.9	Whitehead

Average monthly output (for 6 months ending June 1918)—56 machines.

(b) A Mobilisation Station, for 2 Handley Page Squadrons.

(c) Photographic Experimental Section.

Establishment (for the A.A.P.)

Personnel		Transport	
Officers	33	Touring Cars	2
W.O.s and N.C.O.s above the rank of Corporal	36	Light Tenders	4
		Heavy Tenders	4
Corporals	54	Motor Cycles	3
Rank and File	554	Sidecars	2
Forewomen	3	Trailers (Wing	1
Women	134	(Aeroplane	3
Women (Household)	30	Float Lorries	2
		Ford Chassis	1
		Ambulance	2
		Motor Roller	1
		Workshop Body	2
		Tractors (Ordinary	3
		(Special	1
TOTAL (exclusive of Hostel Staff)	844	TOTAL	31

R.A.F. KENLEY

AERODROME — Maximum dimensions in yards, 1,350 × 850. Area, 174 acres, of which 30 acres are occupied by the Station Buildings. Height above sea level, 550 feet. Soil, heavy clay. Surface, fair. The area in front of the aeroplane sheds get very boggy in wet weather. The ground slopes towards the north and east. General surroundings, heavily timbered and somewhat hilly.

METEOROLOGICAL — The reports for the winter months, October, 1917, to March, 1918, inclusive, for 1,926 daylight hours observed are as follows:

Low Clouds Hours	Rainfall Hours	Wind Hours	Mist Hours	Fog Hours	Possible Flying Hours	Total Hours of Daylight observed	Ratio of Possible Flying to Daylight Hours %	Category
472	371.5	214.5	295.5	100	787	1,926	40.86	4

TENURE POLICY — This station is on the list of permanent stations, though the land is common land.

Accommodation

Technical Buildings

14	Aeroplane Sheds (each 170′ × 80′)
2	Running Sheds
	M.T. Shed
	Technical Stores
	Oil Store
	Petrol Store
	Offices
	Power House
	Latrines
3	Compass Platforms
	Machine Gun Store
2	Gun Butts

Regimental Buildings

	Officers' Mess
4	Officers' Quarters
	Sergeants' Mess
	Sergeants' Latrines
	Regimental Institute
7	Men's Huts
	Men's Baths
	Men's Latrines and Ablution
	Drying Room
	Coal Yard
	Women's Rest Room

STATE OF WORKS AND BUILDINGS — On 1st September, 1918, the percentage of progress was as follows:

		Extensions
Sheds	98	10
Technical Buildings	90	—
Regimental Buildings	100	30
Women's Accommodation—Rest Room only	100	10
Roads	92	5
Water Supply	100	10
Drainage	100	35
Lighting	85	—

The estimated date of completion for the whole station is 31st December, 1918.

In fact, the building programme was not completed until 1919, by which time the Handley Page shed on the western side of Hayes Lane was finished. It is noticeable that there was no mention of the sheds in the Aerodrome Board's Quarterly Survey.

D.H.9As of No 39 Squadron, which was at Kenley in 1922 and 1923. *British Aerospace*

APPENDIX FOUR

Home Defence Duties, 1917

Unlike the Second World War, the control of machines engaged in the air defence of Great Britain during the 1914–18 war was, not surprisingly, primitive, relying mainly on the ability of pilots in the air to read signals spread out on the ground at various landing grounds.

The instructions below were issued to Kenley Aircraft Acceptance Park and others during 1917.

SECRET

OPERATION ORDERS FOR R.F.C. UNITS UNDERTAKING HOME
DEFENCE DUTIES DURING DAYLIGHT RAIDS

"READINESS"
I.

On the Code Word "Readiness" being passed from Home Forces, the Squadron or Flight Telephone Orderly concerned will at once warn all ranks by sounding a succession of short blasts on the Klaxon Horn. On the Klaxon Horn being sounded, or, failing this, the warning "Readiness" being passed, pilots and mechanics will double to the day defence machines. All machines will be brought out of the sheds at the double. Pilots will run engines and await orders. A runner, who will be detailed daily, will proceed to the telephone room to communicate messages to the formation leader.

"PATROL"
II.

On the Code Word "Patrol" being received, machines will ascend in formation, and will proceed climbing on the patrol as detailed by the patrol map, unless a special patrol is ordered by the Officer Commanding, Home Defence Group, Home Forces.

Action
during
patrol
III.

During the patrol, should H.A. be sighted, formation leaders may use their discretion as to engaging them, but it must be borne in mind that the enemy may use single or a small number of machines as a feint, and that therefore they must exercise their discretion in deciding to attack, or in leading their formations in the direction of A.A. shell bursts.

Ground
Signals
IV.

Should Ground Signals be displayed, formation leaders, or machines which have become detached from their formation, will act in accordance.

The last signal observed will be the signal to be acted on and will cancel a signal which may have been observed at the previous Landing Ground. For example: A formation over Landing Ground "A" observes signal to proceed to the N. Foreland; when over Landing Ground "B", the signal to proceed to the Girdler Lightship is observed. In this case, the signal to proceed to the Girdler Lightship will be acted on.

All Clear
V.

On the "All Clear" signal being displayed, machines will land, if possible, at their own aerodromes. If, owing to bad weather conditions, the "All Clear" signal cannot be read, machines will remain on patrol for two hours.

Orders for
placing out
Signals.
VI.

"Signal orders" will only be put out by order of the Officer Commanding, Home Defence Group. In the event of telephonic communication being interrupted Officers Commanding Units will exercise their own discretion in ordering signals to be laid out, reporting any action to the Officer Commanding, Home Defence Group, as soon as telephonic communication is restored.

Detail
VII.

Paras. I–VI of the above orders will apply to No. 39 H.D. Squadron, 37 H.D. Squadron, 50 H.D. Squadron, 78 H.D. Squadron; 46 Squadron; 65 Squadron; 62 T. Squadron; 49 T. Squadron; Acceptance Park, Hendon; Acceptance Park, Lympne; Testing Squadron, Martlesham Heath; Experimental Squadron, Orfordness. Paras I, III, IV, V, VI will apply to Acceptance Park, Kenley Common; 56 T. Squadron; 35 T. Squadron; 40 T. Squadron; 63 T. Squadron; but NOT Para. II; para IX will be substituted for para. II.

Special Orders
to Certain
Units.
VIII.

No. 39 H.D.; No. 46 Squadron; and Acceptance Park, Hendon will not leave their patrol lines unless
(a) Ordered by Signal.
(b) An enemy formation be sighted approaching London.
(c) A.A. fire makes it evident that an H.A. formation is moving on London.
Their special duty is the protection of London from bombing attack.

General
Reserve
IX.

A.P. Kenley Common; 56 T.S.; 35 T.S.; 40 T.S.; 63 T.S.; will be in reserve. Machines from these Units will be kept in a state of readiness on the ground from the time the Code Word "READINESS" is passed until such time as special orders are issued to them, or until the Code Word "ALL

CLEAR" is received; they will not ascend even when receiving "PATROL", their orders to ascend will be given in the Code Words "GENERAL RESERVE PATROL".

H.D. Squadron — Home Defence Squadron
T. Squadron — Training Squadron
H.A. — Hostile Aircraft

MEASURES FOR DEFENCE OF LONDON FROM AEROPLANE RAIDS BY DAY—COMING INTO FORCE 5 A.M. (B.S.T.) AUGUST 11TH 1917.

INSTRUCTIONS — Other fighting machines—all machines available at Croydon, London Colney, Joyce Green, Hendon, Northolt and Kenley Common will rendezvous at 14,000 feet over Joyce Green under a Patrol Leader, specially marked, who will go up from Croydon. While assembling these machines will not go North of Joyce Green.

A 1940 Mystery

How the Dornier Do.17 was brought down during the 18th August, 1940, raid on Kenley has presented aviation historians and diarists with something of a headache dating back to the time the event occurred.

It now appears, through official sources, that several units claimed credit for the unfortunate aircraft's demise. The Scots Guards claimed it for one of their Lewis guns; the 31st Battery, 11th Light Anti-Aircraft Regiment did likewise for one of their Bofors. Eye-witness accounts of having seen the aircraft fly into a Parachute and Cable, then crash, are strongly substantiated by a report by Wing Commander England, who was in charge of the P.A.C. Scheme. On investigation of the wreck he found that the leading edge of the port wing had been cut in a manner which suggested contact with a cable. But the cable and parachute could not be found. It has been put on record that a three-inch shell from one of the guns operated by the 148th Light Anti-Aircraft Battery had struck the Dornier square on the nose and brought it down.

Who was right? The picture remains as clouded as ever. In the heat of the action, any one of them would have been justified in thinking that the credit should go to them if they had been engaging the aircraft; the same principle which led to exaggerated claims for numbers of aircraft destroyed by fighters.

Personnel were not encouraged to stroll around the place and talk about such matters; in fact, because of security precautions, more often than not those on one part of the aerodrome knew little of the workings of another, and so relied on snippets of information for their news, thus no clear picture emerged at the time.

Evidence from the German aircrew would no doubt have been conclusive but they all perished in the crash on "Sunnycroft." Perhaps it was a combination of the two, possibly even three, elements that brought the machine down. We will never know.

One outcome of the Dornier Do.17 incident was that it kept alive the Parachute and Cable production scheme which the Prime Minister, Mr Winston Churchill, was about to terminate. Coincidentally, on the day before the raid he had written to the Secretary of State, Sir Archibald Sinclair, expressing scepticism about the device and concluding that the supply of this particular rocket should be brought to a close in the course of the next month or six weeks, with a minimum of waste of material already assigned to it. After the demonstration of the weapon at Kenley on 22nd August, Churchill changed his mind and the scheme continued, albeit on a much reduced scale.

APPENDIX SIX

Combat Report

It was the strategy of Fighter Command during the Battle of Britain that squadrons from neighbouring Groups should be sent to protect No 11 Group's vulnerable aerodromes when their own fighters were heavily engaged elsewhere, and also to provide cover on such occasions for the aircraft factories to the west of London. It was a policy which did not always work, and led to some criticism from No 11 Group Commander Keith Park about the straying of No 12 Group's squadrons.

The fight in the sky nearly four miles above Croydon and Kenley on 9th September was an action which Nos 19, 310 and 242 Squadrons from No 12 Group, flying as the Duxford "Wing" under Squadron Leader Douglas Bader, were engaged. The Hurricanes involved in the mid-air collision over Purley and that of Pilot Officer Sclanders (No 242 Squadron) who was killed when his aircraft crashed near Birch Wood, Woldingham, were of the "Wing". Sclanders' colleague, Sergeant R. E. V. H. Lonsdale, wrote the following Combat Report on his return to Coltishall, Norfolk, which gives some indication of the ferocity of the teatime battle.

We were ordered to patrol North Weald when approximately 150 enemy aircraft were sighted over London; we approached them and, as the C.O. went into attack, I sighted three 109s coming towards the rear of our formation at approximately a thousand feet below our Squadron. I did a quick turn and made to attack them but could not get into range, so I broke away and found myself on the tails of a formation of Dornier 215s slightly apart from the main formation. I attacked the rearmost machine and gave it a burst of about six seconds and it swung across the formation, then I found I was almost on the tail of another and slightly to one side. I immediately attacked this one and, although my aircraft had been hit several times by heavy cross fire from the rear gunners, I managed to fire all my remaining rounds into him from approximately 200 yards.

I was being repeatedly hit in the engine and controls whilst carrying out this second attack and smoke was coming into my cockpit as well as streams of glycol mixture and oil, also my controls were practically useless except for the elevator. As I broke away from the attack the enemy aircraft had smoke pouring from the fuselage and one engine was smoking badly. I jumped out at about 19,000 feet and finished up in a pine tree in Caterham; my machine landed at Kenley Aerodrome about 200 yards from the Main Guard Room.

The Inspector of Police at Caterham and several soldiers confirmed my report and stated that the machine I was attacking came down some distance away and started to come down at the same time as I jumped out.

There were also other witnesses at Kenley Aerodrome. Whilst dropping slowly to earth, a Spitfire pilot flew round me and stayed with me until I had nearly reached the ground.

Sergeant Lonsdale landed in Harestone Valley Road, Caterham.

The Battle of Britain

Kenley Squadrons

No 64 Squadron
Spitfire

Arrived from Usworth, 16th May, 1940.
Squadron Leader Aeneas MacDonell.
Left for Leconfield, 19th August, 1940.
Aircraft Code SH.
Radio Call Sign   FREEMA.

No 615 Squadron
(County of Surrey)
R.Aux.A.F.
Hurricane

Arrived from Belgium, operational from
  20th May, 1940.
Squadron Leader Joe Kayll.
Left for Prestwick, 30th August, 1940.
Aircraft Code KW.
Radio Call Sign   PANTA.

No 616 Squadron
(South Yorkshire)
R.Aux.A.F.
Spitfire

Arrived from Leconfield, 19th August, 1940.
Squadron Leader Marcus Robinson.
Left for Coltishall, 3rd September, 1940.
Aircraft Code QJ.

No 253 Squadron
(Hyderabad)
Hurricane

Arrived from Prestwick, 30th August, 1940.
Squadron Leader Harold Starr.
Left for Leconfield 3rd January, 1941.
Aircraft Code SW.
Radio Call Sign   VICEROY.

No 66 Squadron
Spitfire

Arrived from Coltishall, 3rd September, 1940.
Squadron Leader Rupert Leigh.
Left for Gravesend, 11th September, 1940.
Aircraft Code LZ.
Radio Call Sign   FIBUS

No 501 Squadron
(County of Gloucester)
R.Aux.A.F.
Hurricane

Arrived from Gravesend, 10th September, 1940.
Squadron Leader Harry Hogan.
Left for Filton, 17th December, 1940.
Aircraft Code SD.
Radio Call Sign   MANDREL.

Kenley Radio Call Sign then in use — RUNIK.

The Cost of the Battle of Britain

Losses in combat of men and machines from Kenley during the period July–October 1940.

PILOTS

No 64 Squadron — 5

25th July	Flying Officer A. J. O. Jeffery lost in Channel off Dover.
,, ,,	Sub-Lieutenant Dawson Paul crashed in Channel (died 30th).
5th August	Sergeant L. R. Isaac shot down over Channel.
8th ,,	Pilot Officer Kennard-Davis baled out, died 10th August Royal Victoria Hospital, Dover.
15th ,,	Flying Officer C. J. D. Andreae killed in combat over Channel.

No 615 Squadron — 5

14th July	Pilot Officer Mudie shot down into Channel, picked up by Royal Navy, died next day.
14th August	Flying Officer P. Collard shot down in Channel off Dover.
,, ,,	Pilot Officer C. R. Montgomery shot down in Channel off Dover. Intercepting raid by Ju.87s on Folkestone Lightship.
15th ,,	Sergeant D. W. Hatton shot down by Me.109.
18th ,,	Sergeant P. K. Walley crashed Morden Park.

No 616 Squadron — 4

25th August	Sergeant Westmoreland killed intercepting raid over Canterbury.
26th ,,	Sergeant M. Ridley shot down over Deal–Dover area by Me.109s.
,, ,,	Flying Officer Moberly shot down over Deal–Dover area by Me.109s.
30th ,,	Pilot Officer J. S. Bell shot down by Me.109s, crashed West Malling.

No 253 Squadron — 10

30th August	Pilot Officer C. D. Francis shot down in combat with Me.109s. Crashed near Wrotham, Kent.
„ „	Pilot Officer D. N. O. Jenkins shot down in combat over Redhill by fighters. Baled out but was shot out of parachute by Me.109 pilot over Woldingham.
„ „	Sergeant J. H. Dickinson shot down in combat over Dungeness. Baled out but killed.
31st „	Squadron Leader Harold Starr shot down by enemy fighters over Kent.
1st September	Pilot Officer J. K. G. Clifton shot down in combat over Dungeness.
4th „	Flying Officer A. A. G. Trueman shot down in combat over base.
6th „	Acting Sub-Lieutenant Cambridge baled out, killed.
14th „	Sergeant W. B. Higgins crashed after clash with Me.109s.
26th „	Pilot Officer W. M. C. Samolinski lost over Channel.
10th October	Sergeant H. H. Allgood crashed at Maidstone.

No 66 Squadron — 2

4th September	Sergeant A. D. Smith shot down over Ashford, died two days later.
5th „	Flying Officer R. J. C. King shot down in combat with Me.109s. Baled out but parachute failed to open.

No 501 Squadron — 7

15th September	Pilot Officer A. E. A. Van den Hove d'Ertsenryck, while attacking Dornier 17s, set upon by Me.109s over Kent.
17th „	Sergeant Egan shot down over Ashford during dogfight with Me.109s.
27th „	Pilot Officer E. M. Gunter, while attacking force of Dornier 17s, was attacked by Me.109s. Baled out but parachute failed to open.
28th „	Pilot Officer F. C. Harrold shot down by Me.109s near Deal.
7th October	Flying Officer N. J. M. Barry shot down by Me.109.
15th „	Sergeant S. A. Fenemore shot down during dogfight with Me.109s over Redhill.
25th „	Pilot Officer V. Goth killed in mid-air collision with Pilot Officer MacKenzie during combat with Me.109s.

All of these pilots lost their lives; there were many others who were wounded.

AIRCRAFT (Lost or damaged beyond repair)

No 64 Squadron	9 Spitfires
No 615 Squadron	13 Hurricanes
No 616 Squadron	13 Spitfires
No 253 Squadron	23 Hurricanes
No 66 Squadron	6 Spitfires
No 501 Squadron	16 Hurricanes

On 26th August No 616 Squadron lost seven Spitfires, now believed to be the largest number of aircraft totally lost (none was repairable) by any British squadron in a single day of the battle. Three forced landed, two crashed, two shot down into the sea. All were victims of Messerschmitt Bf.109s, who caught one Section while they were still climbing. The vital tactical lessons learned that day were not wasted on one of the Squadron's pilots. He writes:

> There were two basic problems facing inexperienced Fighter Squadrons arriving in 11 Group in August and September, 1940. Firstly all training in fighter tactics had been based on tight formation in sections of three, and no flexibility was allowed; consequently all except the leader had to concentrate on formation flying and were very vulnerable to being "jumped".
>
> Secondly, Fighter Command policy was to conserve Squadrons by delaying ordering them to "scramble" until they had identified the main thrust of the raid and by the end of August this meant the bomber force.
>
> This inevitably meant that Squadrons were "scrambled" from their bases in 11 Group to meet the incoming bombers which resulted in their going into action while still climbing and often with the sun behind the German aircraft. Until Squadron Commanders appreciated this and switched to a loose formation based on a unit of two, and at the same time manoeuvred to get height and sun advantage, Squadrons such as 616 had very heavy casualties.
>
> Once the lessons were learnt, pilots started to be successful and Squadron losses became more acceptable.

> Group Captain Denys Gillam, D.S.O. 2 Bars, D.F.C. 1 Bar, A.F.C.
> (Then a flight lieutenant with the squadron)

What of Luftwaffe losses during this period? From the German point of view, perhaps this can best be summarised by a particularly poignant passage in German fighter ace Adolf Galland's excellent book *The First and the Last*. In chapter three, titled "A battle for life and death", he writes:

> We saw one comrade after the other, old and tested brothers in combat, vanish from the ranks. Not a day passed without a place remaining empty at the Mess table. New faces appeared, became familiar, until one day these too would disappear, shot down in the Battle of Britain.*

I am indebted to Peter Cornwell for his assistance in compiling this list. The results of his many years of dedicated research on the subject can be seen in the book *The Battle of Britain, Then and Now.*

*By kind permission of Franz Schneekluth Verlag, Munich.

APPENDIX NINE

Houses Requisitioned

During the Second World War the demands of expansion and security led to dispersion and many local houses were requisitioned. Among those taken over were the following:

1939	Hillhurst, Salmons Lane	W.A.A.F. Mess (later Sick Quarters)
1940	High House, Whyteleafe Road	Station Headquarters
1941	Peterswood, Torwood Lane	Station Headquarters
1940	The Oaks, Carshalton	Emergency Operations Room
1940	Spice & Wallis' butcher's shop, 11 Godstone Road, Caterham	Operations Room
1940	The Grange, Canons Hill, Old Coulsdon	Operations Room
1940	The Crest, Hayes Lane	Detachment Headquarters Scots Guards and gunpost (destroyed by Luftwaffe 18th August, 1940)
1941	Bleak House, Torwood Lane	Station Accounts
1940	Portley Lodge, Whyteleafe	Officers' Mess
1940	Salmons, Whyteleafe Road	Commanding Officer's Headquarters
1942	The Turret, Whyteleafe Road, Caterham	Theatre and Chapel
1939	Grove House, Salmons Lane	W.A.A.F. Quarters
1940	Coulsdon Court Golf Course clubhouse	Mess and Social Centre
	Greenlands and Mayfly Cottage in Buxton Lane were purchased many years earlier by the R.A.F.	W.A.A.F. Quarters

Many other private houses in the district were taken over for R.A.F. billets.

Kenley Squadrons and Aircraft

Dates shown are when the squadron officially moved (in peacetime) or the date of the movement of the bulk of the squadron's aircraft (in wartime), where this did not coincide with the main ground party.

Squadron	Dates	Aircraft
No 1	5.1.41 to 7.4.41 1.6.41 to 14.6.41	Hurricane
No 1 (Communication)	–.4.19 to –.9.19	D.H.4A, Handley Page 0/400
No 3	10.5.34 to 4.10.35 28.8.36 to 2.5.39 28.1.40 to 10.5.40 20.5.40 to 23.5.40	Bulldog, Gladiator, Hurricane
No 13	1.4.24 to 30.6.24	Bristol Fighter F2B
No 17	10.5.34 to 23.5.39 24.5.40 to 6.6.40	Hart, Bulldog, Gauntlet, Hurricane
No 23	6.2.27 to 17.9.32	Gamecock, Bulldog, Hart, Demon
No 24 (Communication)	7.1.20 to 15.1.27	Avro 504K, D.H.9A, Bristol Fighter, Snipe, Fawn
No 32	1.4.23 to 30.6.24 (Re-formed) 5.8.24 to 21.9.32	Snipe, Gamecock, Siskin IIIA, Bulldog IIA, Grebe
No 36	12.6.30 to 28.6.30 (Detached from Donibristle)	Hawker Horsley
No 39	18.1.22 to 8.2.23	D.H.9A
No 46	3.9.36 to 15.11.37	Gauntlet
No 64	16.5.40 to 19.8.40	Spitfire
No 66	3.9.40 to 11.9.40 13.8.43 to 17.9.43	Spitfire
No 80	8.3.37 to 15.3.37	Gauntlet
No 84	–.1.20 to 30.1.20	S.E.5A
No 88	–.4.18 to 20.4.18	Bristol Fighter F2B
No 91	4.7.18 to 3.7.19	Sopwith Dolphin
No 95	1.10.18 to –.11.18	Formation of squadron abandoned before aircraft were received.

No 108	14.6.18 to 22.7.18	D.H.9
No 110	15.6.18 to 1.9.18	D.H.9A
No 111	28.7.42 to 21.9.42	Spitfire
No 165	8.8.43 to 17.9.43	Spitfire
No 253	8.5.40 to 24.5.40 29.8.40 to 3.1.41	Hurricane
No 258 (Polish)	21.4.41 to 10.6.41	Hurricane
No 302 (Polish)	7.4.41 to 29.5.41	Hurricane
No 312 (Belgian)	29.5.41 to 20.7.41	Hurricane
No 350	16.7.42 to 31.7.42	Spitfire
No 401 (Canadian)	23.9.42 to 23.1.43	Spitfire
No 402 (Canadian)	14.5.42 to 31.5.42 13.8.42 to 21.3.43	Spitfire
No 403 (Canadian)	23.1.43 to 7.8.43 14.10.43 to 24.2.44 29.2.44 to 18.4.44	Spitfire
No 411	27.3.43 to 7.4.43	Spitfire
No 412 (Canadian)	1.11.42 to 24.11.42	Spitfire
No 416 (Canadian)	1.2.43 to 29.5.43 11.2.44 to 14.4.44	Spitfire
No 421 (Canadian)	30.1.43 to 1.3.43 12.3.43 to 24.3.43 18.5.43 to 5.8.43 14.10.43 to 24.2.44	Spitfire
No 452 (R.A.A.F.)	21.7.41 to 21.10.41 14.1.42 to 23.3.42	Spitfire
No 485 (New Zealand)	21.10.41 to 8.7.42	Spitfire
No 501	10.9.40 to 17.12.40	Hurricane
No 600	1.10.38 to 3.10.38	Demon
No 602	10.7.41 to 14.1.42 4.3.42 to 13.5.42	Spitfire
No 611	3.6.42 to 13.7.42	Spitfire
No 615	1.6.37 to 29.8.38 4.9.38 to 2.9.39 20.5.40 to 29.8.40 17.12.40 to 21.4.41	Tutor, Hector, Gauntlet, Gladiator, Hurricane
No 616	19.8.40 to 3.9.40 8.7.42 to 29.7.42	Spitfire

General Index

Illustrations in bold type

Ranks shown are those relevant at the time of the event

GENERAL INDEX

Lister, Flying Officer Pat, 43
Lofts, Pilot Officer, 68, 69, 77
Longman, Sergeant, 97
Lonsdale, Sergeant R., 97, 168
Looker, Pilot Officer D., 77, 80
Lowe, Flight Lieutenant C. N., 25
Luxmoore, Flying Officer F. L., 23, 25
Lympne aerodrome, 9, 34

M
MacDonell, Squadron Leader Aeneas "Don", 58, 64, 78, 109, 169
Mackay, Group Captain E. P., 40
Mackenzie, Wing Commander S., 146
MacKenzie, Pilot Officer K. W., 106, 107
Macpherson, Mr (Under Secretary for War), 3
Magwood, Flight Lieutenant, 141
Mansell, Squadron Leader Rex, 37
Manston aerodrome, 19, 48, 73, 126
Marden D/F Station, 52
Marshal, Mrs Hilda, 74
Martyn, Squadron Leader, 40
Mason, Group Captain N. W. F., 34
Mathy, Captain Heinrich, 5
Maxwell, Squadron Leader R. S., 27
May, Pilot Officer Henry, 43
McCallum, Major, 9, 14
McClintock, Pilot Officer, 77
McCrindle, Mr, 18
McDonald, Air Commodore A. W. B., 36
McEvoy, Air Chief Marshal Sir Theodore, 26, 148
McKellar, Flight Lieutenant Archie, 99, 100
Merton Technical College, 78
Military Aeronautics Directorate (War Office), 1
Miller, Lance-Corporal J., 70, 85
Mobile Disarmament Units, 146
Montgomery, Pilot Officer C. R., 60
Montgomery, Pilot Officer (32 Squadron), 32
Morrow, Sergeant H., 141
Mudie, Pilot Officer, 82
Murch, Pilot Officer, 101

N
Neville, C. W., 35
Newton, Sergeant Harry (later Squadron Leader), 65, 76, 149
Nicholl, Major H. R., 14
Night interception experiment, 112
Noel, Captain, 4
Norman, Squadron Leader A., 64
Northolt aerodrome, 25, 26, 27, 35, 59, 168
North Weald aerodrome, 47
Nuffield, Lord, 127

O
Observer Corps, 41, 51, 52, 53, 64, 69, 78, 87, 100, 101, 102, 111, 142
Old Sarum aerodrome, 42
Owen-Edmunds, Pilot Officer D., 64, 78
Owens, Arthur, 63, 118

P
Parachute and Cable (P.A.C.), 55, 70, 73, 86, 167

Paris Peace Conference at Versailles, 16
Park, Air Vice-Marshal Keith, 59, 60, 87, 98, 100, 168
Peel, Wing Commander John, 119, 125
Pevensey radar station, 62
Pickup, Squadron Leader, 145
"Pip squeak", 53, 90, 103, 112, 127
Pitcher, Flying Officer, 24
P.O.W.s (German), 147
Prestwick aerodrome, 88, 169
Prickman, Wing commander Thomas, 57, 149, 150
Primrose, Air Commodore W. H., 18

Q
Queen's Royal Regiment 55, 83

R
Raab, Feldwebel Wilhelm, 70
Radar A.I. (Air Interception), 111, 112, 113, 119
R.A.F. Regiment, 55
R.A.F. Volunteer Reserve, 43, 44, 48
Ramer, Captain (U.S.A.A.F.), 137
Raymond, Cyril, 148
Reay, H. M., 9
Redhill aerodrome, 51, 80, 108, 111, 119, 120, 128
Reid, Stephen, 64, 73, 74
Robb, Flight Lieutenant James, 23–25, **27**, 37
Roberts, Aircraftman Second Class D., 70
Robinson, Squadron Leader Marcus, 169
Rose, Pilot Officer, 49
Rose and Crown Riddlesdown, 17, 105
Roth, Hauptmann Joachim, 64, 69
Roux, Gene, 69
Royal Aircraft Factory, Farnborough, 1
Royal Defence Corps, 11
Royal Engineers, 83, 84
Royal Fusiliers, 12th Battalion, 48
Runways, 158
Russell, Major, 112
Rust, Pamela (W.A.A.F.), 115
Ryder, Wing Commander Norman, 126

S
Salmond, Sir John, 18, **27**
Samson, Air Commodore C. R., 26, 29, 32
Sanders, Flight Lieutenant, 57, 58, 77, 87
Sawyer, Joseph, 22
Sclanders, Pilot Officer, 168
Scots Guards, 55, 61, 70
Scott, Group Captain A. F. L., 25
Scott, C. W. A., 26
Searchlights, 112
Shackerby, Mr, 74
Sheldrake, Reg, 149
Sholto Douglas, Air Marshal Sir William, **128**
Shoreham aerodrome, 51
Simpson, Pilot Officer Peter, 65, 75, 76
Sinclair, Pilot Officer G. L., 96
Skegg, Peter, 70, 85
Sopwith, T. O. M., 11

178

Index of Aeroplanes